SKIPPER VS CREW, CREW VS SKIPPER

Strifes, stresses and strains
between crew and skipper!

TIM DAVISON

Illustrations by John Quirk

ADLARD COLES NAUTICAL

B L O O M S B U R Y
LONDON · NEW DELHI · NEW YORK · SYDNEY

CONTENTS ⚓

CREW vs SKIPPER

For Mike Peyton, who taught me that sailing is too important to be taken seriously.

INTRODUCTION

The inevitable war between skipper and crew makes scrummaging in the Rugby World Cup look like a picnic. After all, when the going gets tough ashore, one protagonist can go to the pub. On a boat there's no escape – you just have to slug it out.

This book aims to take the conflict to a higher level, but is even-handed in its advice.

The bumptious skipper will of course read from the front (casually assuming the book is written for him). Here he will find new and exciting ways to exploit those forward of the tiller, and much to reinforce his guiding principle (culled from *Mushroom Grower's Weekly*): 'If you want them to mature keep them in the dark, keep them wet and keep them away from home soil'.

Meanwhile the crew, programmed to find more subtle ways round problems, will be reading from the back. Here they'll find an arsenal of weapons to turn the tide and win the war. Remember, from his position on Fantasy Island, the skipper is completely helpless. Shout as much as he likes, only the crew can hoist and lower sails, tend the sheets and fend off when it all goes wrong. Read on, you honest matelots, to gain the upper hand ...

THE CREW'S RULES

RULE 1
If there are two possible harbours, we prefer the nearer. Unless we're sunbathing.

RULE 2
We're not mind readers. Tell us what you want. Then accept what we decide to do.

RULE 3
Saying 'Please' is not a sign of weakness.

RULE 4
If the skipper's paying we'll eat ashore. If not, it's his turn to cook.

RULE 5
This is an equal opportunity boat. We like steering. You will find cleaning the loo very fulfilling.

RULE 6
Shouting is the last refuge of a frightened man. Unless we've already abandoned ship, in which case do shout to tell us how to activate the EPIRB.

RULE 7
If the sail cover protects the mainsail from the sun, why do we have to put it on 'for the night'?

RULE 8
How come you shout at us for not turning off the gas, but expect to get away with leaving it on 'so it's ready for the next person'?

RULE 9
Don't treat victualling as an opportunity to clear out stuff from home that's past its sell by date. Go to Tesco like the other skippers.

RULE 10
Welcome sarcastic banter as a contribution to ship's morale, e.g.:

SKIPPER	Can you fix that genoa leech?
CREW	Certainly.
SKIPPER	By trimming it or easing it?
CREW	By ripping it.

WORLD RECORDS

THE LONGEST HELMSMAN'S RANT

The longest recorded piece of crew criticism was an incredible rant lasting 3 hr 45 min 15 sec by John Foulmouth while berating his crew for dropping a winch handle overboard. The record took place in Dover Harbour on 15 June 2003. He was later flown to hospital and spent the night in an oxygen tent before being discharged. He now sails singlehanded.

LONGEST PERIOD WITHOUT ORDERS

With a time of 6 min 45.3 sec, Fred Meek set a new record for remaining silent, but was eventually unable to refrain from asking the crew to pull in the genoa a smidge, move so he could see the echosounder, and put the kettle on. The record was made on 25 May 1999 at Cork, Ireland.

MOST COLLISIONS

Fred Dingworthy, who was 91 at the time, set the record for the most collisions in an hour. Mr Dingworthy was on a weekend cruise but inadvertently reached down the startline for the Round the Island Race off Cowes, an error caused by his hat slipping down over his eyes. He hit 153 boats, 1223 sailors were involved and a staggering £4.7 million of damage done. His insurance company presented him with a free membership to his local bowls club in the hope that he would change sport. When he refused they raised the excess on his policy to £20 million.

Fred Dingworthy in action ...

LONGEST DISTANCE SAILED BACKWARDS

The longest reverse was 335.2 miles and was achieved at the Bangor Annual Regatta (Ireland) in June 2010 by David Sternboard (USA). He went head-to-wind at the start and was unable to get out of irons, eventually being rescued two days later at Lands End. But, having mastered the art of sailing backwards, he is now building a new boat with the rudder at the bow and will attempt a reverse circumnavigation of the world.

SHORTEST RACE

Hans Landlock (Switzerland) made history in the 1996 Uber Cup when he hit the committee boat 2.8 seconds after the start and sank. The yacht had taken a year to build and cost £6 million, or £2 million per second of her racing life.

HIGHEST SCORE IN ANTIFOUL EVENTING

Won by Jim Leach at the Bottom Boatyard in March 2011, the competition consists of three disciplines: Costume design; Bottom sanding; Paintball duelling.

Mr Leach scored a 10 (max) for his overalls, which he wore while rolling in a mix of mud, antifouling and thinner. The judges may have been swayed by his looking like a cute chocolate bunny.

He sanded a standard hull in just 6.3 min by driving a flock of sheep underneath it. They had been fed on an iron-rich diet and their backs were covered in iron wool.

In the paintball section Jim chose to fire old socks dipped in coppercoat from a modified ship's foghorn. The combination of sound and thrust was too much for the other competitors and he won the knockout competition easily.

THE SLEEPIEST SKIPPER

The record for snoozing while in charge is 23 hr 49 min set by Tim Eider-Down on 29 June 2012 on his Bavaria *Somnambulist*. He slept through Force 10, a dismasting, a 360 degree roll and hitting a rock, finally waking up in the rescue helicopter clutching his teddy and complaining about a lumpy pillow.

FASTEST ONBOARD DASH

In this event the contestants line up in the water 100 m from the boat and the start is signalled by the release of a rubber shark. The winner is the fastest person to swim to the boat, climb the boarding ladder and shoot the shark. (It is a disqualifiable offence to shoot other competitors who are still swimming.)

The current world record is 9.9 sec held by Hans Walkwater (Australia) in the Whitsunday Islands event of 2001. At the start two sharks surfaced, the rubber one and a Great White. Mr Walkwater had the presence of mind to mount the rubber shark, pull out the plug and be jetted to the yacht as it deflated. Unfortunately his shooting was poor and the judges are still piecing together the chewed remains of the other competitors.

HIGHEST NUMBER OF FAILED NAVIGATION EXAMS

Navigation student Vasco da Smith has still to pass Elementary Navigation, gaining a grade F on no fewer than 231 occasions. On 27 of these he was unable to find the exam room. He flunked the oral 123 times with errors that have since passed into folklore, such as telling the examiner that Leeway means that exam marking is flexible, a parallel rule is a feature of The Coalition, interpolate is a European Police Agency and EP was a space oddity.

His other problems were in the practical: he gave his Dead Reckoning position as 'I've probably got a good 25 years left' and refused to take a fix on the grounds of his recent drug addiction.

Nonetheless, Mr da Smith sails regularly in and around Folkestone harbour and up the M20.

LONGEST SKIPPER'S BRIEFING

On 23 April 2004 skipper John Loquacious briefed his crew for an agonising 2 days 8 hr 38 min on board his 27ft *Purple Yawn*. Most of this was a monologue about his views on safety, weather forecasting etc., but over 5 hours were taken up trying to recover a fender in the Man Overboard demonstration (it was eventually abandoned). No one could find the lifejackets or flares, necessitating a 24-mile trip to a chandler, the toilet was jammed so the boat had to be lifted out and a new seacock fitted, and the gas hissed straight into the bilge rather than through the burners. The final 24 hours were spent persuading the crew that they really did want to come on the cruise with him...

MOST G & TS CONSUMED IN THE COCKPIT

On 29 April 1999 the crew of the maxi *Bombay Sapphire Preprandial* downed an amazing 36.7 litres of gin in 60 min while celebrating a win in Antigua Raceweek. The also got through 42.3 litres of tonic, 56 kilos of ice and 721 lemons, most of which were thrown at other yachts moored nearby.

LOWEST BODY TEMPERATURE

Lee Dropoff (USA) achieved the lowest body temperature while on watch in a 1987 crossing from Iceland to Norway. The temperature in her boots dropped to -38 deg C and her toes were measured at -6 deg C (23 deg F).

Her watch-mate saved the day by pouring a litre of warm soup into each wellie and telling her stories about bargain-hunting in Tiffany's.

LONGEST VHF CALL

Jan Johnston (Arg) inadvertently sent the longest ever call on Channel 16 when she replaced the handset with the PTT button pressing against the wall. *Soliloquy*'s radio broadcast every sound from the boat for 6 days 17 hr 34 min, including discussions about the commodore's bankruptcy, arguments about the skipper's sanity and heavy breathing from the fo'c'sle. The call continued to block the emergency channel until a frigate was sent to shoot away the VHF aerial from the top of the mast.

LIGHTEST KITBAG

The lightest bag brought on board weighed 26 grams and contained only a spare pair of underpants. The owner, Sid Smelley, was forced to make spare clothes and oilskins from the galley's bacofoil.

HEAVIEST KITBAG

A valise weighing 1456 kg was winched aboard the 17m ketch *Displacement* on 6 July 1976. It contained among other things a spare toilet, a dishwasher, a wheelbarrow and parts for the ship's Aga. It was stowed in the stern cabin, curing at one stroke the boat's tendency to nosedive on the run.

MOST JOKES TOLD IN A TWO-HOUR WATCH

'Mad' Jock McKnee (Scotland) told a total of 676 jokes on *Jester*'s 2–4 am watch on 21 September 2010*. The starboard watch, below at the time but unable to sleep, declared the cockpit henceforth a joke-free zone. The following night they fixed him up with a snorkel mouthpiece attached via a tube to a bottle of whisky, which kept him quiet until he passed out shortly before dawn.

To see how bad it was, consider the following:

Q. *How many skippers does it take to open a beer?*
A. None, he expects it to be open when the crew bring it to him.

A skipper kneels by a graveside silently weeping. The crew are a respectful distance away. They hear him sob 'Why, why, oh why did you have to die?' They're amazed, he is normally a ruthless character. This goes on for a while. Finally, all is made clear when they hear him mutter: 'If only you had lived, the boat wouldn't have been sold and I wouldn't have been the idiot to buy her. And have to sail with that lot of reprobates ...'

MOST TOILET BLOCKAGES ON A WEEKEND CRUISE

The heads on the sloop *Gutrot* were cleared 14 times in a 48 hour period from 24–26 December 2011. Blockages included an orange, a lump of coal, a Father Christmas beard and a foghorn. No crew member is now allowed to use the heads without first taking off their shoes and belt, putting their laptop on the chart table and passing through security.

THE FASTEST TRIP TO THE HEADS

John Strippenburg managed a spirited exit from the cockpit, removed lifejacket, outer-, mid- and inner layers, visited the heads, got dressed again and was back on the helm a staggering 45 seconds later. He attributed his speed to consuming earlier two kilos of liquorice allsorts.

LONELY HEARTS OF OAK

In our Advice Column for sailors our Agony Aunt, sea-kindly Eileen Dover(!), answers letters from people suffering the same problems as you.

I WANT A BOAT!

Dear Eileen

I am 30 and have been crewing for 5 years on other people's boats. Although fairly new to sailing I can tie knots, stand a watch and pour drinks at sea. I am getting to the stage where I want a boat of my own before it's too late: I can almost feel my clock ticking.

A mortuary technician's dream ...

My problem is that I am unsure of my navigation and don't have enough friends to crew any yacht I could afford – I should mention that I'm a mortuary technician, which seems dead boring to most people. I guess I can spend about £6000.

I haven't mentioned this burning ache to my girlfriend, who hates sailing anyway. Please help me decide what to do!

Confused of Portsmouth

Dear Confused

I am so sorry you are suffering in this way. But cheer up, many people dream of yachts for years before buying one, when their dream turns to the nightmare of selling her on before the osmosis becomes too obvious.

You suggest a lack of friends is holding you back, and this is possibly because you spend your days surrounded by corpses. Try to spend more time with people who are alive, and preferably look good in oilskins.

I promise your self confidence will grow if you talk less about cremation and learn to love yourself.

You will obviously need a long talk with your girlfriend. Try to be empathic, but if you feel she will never be happy at sea consider getting rid of her, joining a navigation class and chatting up the most attractive student. Failing that, go for the one who understands secondary ports. In the rare case where no one is attractive or tidal, maybe you can use some formaldehyde from work to anaesthetise members of your local yacht club before press-ganging them into service.

Before employing these tactics, it may be best to get a boat first. Do check that the seller really owns her, the sails go up and down and the hull floats. On your budget, this is probably all you can expect.

Always remember you are a unique individual and deserve to be a boat owner and I am sure you will succeed.

I wish you well.

Eileen

MY CREW WON'T SAY WHAT'S WRONG

I get the feeling my crew aren't being honest with me. They've been in a funny mood for weeks but when I ask why, they say nothing's wrong. My mind's working overtime – are they being wooed by another skipper? Do they plan to buy their own boat? Will they still be coming on the annual cruise?

How can I move forward: the uncertainty is driving me crazy.

Brian, Cork

Dear Brian

Your imagination is running riot, but there may be a simple explanation. Perhaps your installing a swearbox on the foredeck hasn't gone down well? Maybe pairing Samantha and Jonathan in the quarterberth is disturbing the other off-watch sleepers? Was doing a Man Overboard practice at 3 am really necessary?

When the chips are really down that (unpopular) MOB practice will pay off ...

Unless you communicate you may never know. Sit everyone down in the saloon and ask for suggestions on clearing the air (ignore facetious ideas like cutting it with a knife or putting bleach down the heads). If your little docking problem comes up, remind them that the jetty has now been repaired and the harbourmaster's car re-sprayed.

Encourage positive contributions: I'm sure they will be very enthusiastic about maintenance weekends in the winter and delighted to chip in for the antifouling.

Point out that you'd rather know the truth than deal with the worry of not knowing. (But be ready to turn down suggestions that you re-sit the Certificate of Competence, shower twice daily or request a 'frequent user' card from the rescue services.) You are the skipper, after all.

Yours

Eileen

COULD I BE BANKRUPT?

Dear Eileen

Lightning has destroyed the electronics, we've ripped the genoa and the spinnaker, bent the rudder and flooded the engine. And that was just the first weekend!

It's early in the season and I forgot to renew the insurance. Now I'm dreading the yard bill and fear I may be insolvent. Please help me!

Sam, Derby

Dear Sam

You are either accident prone or a rotten sailor. Either way, it may be best to consider another hobby, preferably one where you wear padded clothing and remain in your armchair.

Reading between the lines, it sounds as if you are determined to keep the boat, so steel yourself, something will have to go. In fact most owners find that nearly everything has to go.

Firstly, take stock of your assets. I'm not talking about a cute nose and a walk-on part in Jack and the Beanstalk. Your house, car, life insurance etc. are what sailors normally sacrifice.

Next, work out your income. Maybe you can earn more if you spend less time sanding, varnishing and reading yachting magazines in the shed?

Then calculate your monthly expenditure. Is more than 70% marine related?

Finally, write for my factsheet Scheme Your Way to Success: How to Become a Breton Plotter.

Accident prone or a chip off the old block?

Armed with this data, you're ready to assess the problem.

Good hunting!

Eileen

DO I LOVE THIS BOAT?

Dear Eileen

I'm smitten with a 32ft wooden sloop at brokerage in our local yard. I can't get her out of my mind. She seems beautiful to my eye. Should I buy her?

Tom, Aberdeen

Dear Tom

Oh dear, you have got it bad. You're in love with the boat!

Research shows there are different types of love. In your childhood your Optimist was everything to you. Later, you valued the reliable family Wayfarer, your passport to the adult world of club sailing. Then came the thrill of racing a trapeze/spinnaker boat – I'm sure you can remember the first time you planed downwind in a big sea, survived the gybe, thrashed back upwind and took the gun – you felt like you owned the world.

But these feelings are infatuation. They simply cannot last and eventually reality breaks through. The things that you valued – the lightness of hull, the huge sail area, the large fleets – become the very things you despise as you capsize for the nth time and wait an age for the rescue boat.

No, if you and your boat are to spend a lifetime together you need lasting qualities like thick fibreglass, stainless fittings and one careful previous owner.

Now go back and look at your intended with open eyes.

And remember, she may be perfect but always start with a low offer ...

Your friend in need

Eileen

I THINK HE'S FALLING FOR ANOTHER BOAT

Dear Eileen

My skipper Paul and I have been cruising our Westerley for several years. Actually he's a rotten helmsman, but I've learned how to compensate. Latterly his mood has changed and I'm worried that he may be cheating on us. Last week a 'friend' phoned to say she had seen him racing a dinghy on Wednesday evenings. I asked Paul about this but he refused to discuss it apart from saying that the Westerley is the only boat for him.

I've asked him to come to the marina on Wednesdays but he always says he has to work late, then arrives at closing time smelling of beer and soggy wetsuit. I also found lipstick on his lifejacket. Is this the end of our happy cruising?

Sue, Liverpool

Dear Sue

Try to put a positive slant on your worries. It's almost impossible to get up to much in a full wetsuit and his new crew won't be impressed if the après sail consists of drinking beer and discussing the luffing rules.

When the novelty has worn off I am sure he will get fed up with spending a fortune on ballbearing fittings and Kevlar sails while still coming last.

Also, a bit of close racing should improve his helming skills so you run aground less often and might actually make ground to windward.

Take that Creative Ropework course, buy a new anorak and some tight Dubarry boots, turn up the Eberspacher and look forward to renewed conviviality in your snug cabin.

Goodnight

Eileen

I DON'T SEA WHAT YOU MEAN

Skippers and crew seem to have difficulty understanding each other, so the stage is set for a whole range of nautical blunders. For those who find it hard to read between the lines, or even to know if it's a line they're hearing, here's a quick crib.

WHAT THE CREW SAYS	WHAT THE CREW MEANS
Size doesn't matter	Anything over 50 feet (and with two heads) will do
Does the boat have two heads?	There's a chance one will be working
Can I hold the torch?	My first husband would have got that going ages ago
Rice with diced sausage. Yum yum!	Pity Sue isn't on board. Her Thai curry was fantastic
Bit lively today	Sorry I spilt the soup in your wellies
How much water do the tanks hold?	Are you going to be mean on showers?
Should I bring anything?	If I don't it'll be cheese sarnies and beer all weekend
Is John bringing his girlfriend?	I could use some sensible conversation
How do the finances work?	I'm not chipping in to keep this disaster area afloat
What height do you want the fenders?	How do you tie a clove hitch again?
Pass the bucket	Your jokes are making me sick
You must be very proud of her	Why does owning 32ft of fibreglass imply mastery of the universe?
The Cruising Guide says Comfort Creek is snug in this wind direction	Otherwise we'll have to thrash to windward for another four hours

NACRONYMS (NAUTICAL ACRONYMS)

In this age of texting and emailing, and the hurry of modern life, people are using acronyms more and more, and the nautical world is bound to follow. Think of it as a modern-day form of signalling.

Here are some common acronyms, with their new nautical meaning:

GBH (Grievous Bodily Harm)	Gooseneck Broken. Help!
KISS (Keep It Simple, Stupid)	Knots Impossible. Substitute Shackles
WLTM (Would Like To Meet)	Waves Large, Taking Medicine
DHSS (Dep. Health & Social Security)	Developed Haemorrhoids, Stopped Sailing
FHB (Family Hold Back)	Food Hardly Bearable
RSJ (Reinforced Steel Joist)	Ripped the S*dding Jib
GSOH (Good Sense of Humour)	Good Sailor, Own House
TLC (Tender Loving Care)	Totally Lethal Crew
BBC (British Broadcasting Corporation)	Boat Broaching Continuously
NATO (North Atlantic Treaty Organisation)	Navigating Around Tidal Overfalls
BFN (Bye For Now)	Blowing Force 9
GPS (Global Positioning System)	Get Paralytic Soon

Having got the idea, you should be ready for some altogether new ones:

PSHAW	Pottering Slowly, Hardly Any Wind
SISS	Skipper Insane, Send Shrink
CISS	Crew Impossible, Send Straightjackets
BISS	Boat Iffy, Send Shipwright
FLAGS	Fantastic Lasagne And Great Seafood
OCS (ref racing)	On Course Side
OCS (ref jokes onboard)	On Coarse Side
OCS (ref Samantha on the foredeck)	On Cor! Side
AIWWA	Any Idea Where We Are?
NITS	Not In Timbuktu, Surely
SHAFT	Sunny Hot And Force 3
ASSAM	Abandoning Ship Soon, Alert Mother
HOLDALL	Helicopter Overhead Lowering Doughnuts, And Lifeboat Launched

So a modern text might look something like this:

In Med. Were PSHAW, then BFN. BBC, SISS, CISS, BISS. Luckily Samantha
OCS and cooking FLAGS. WLTM, ASSAM. XX

Eliciting the reply:

Lucky! Here FHB. New squeeze GSOH, but DHSS. Bit OCS!
Already HOLDALL. Mother says you can GPS. XOX

Simple, really!

OLD MIKE AND THE BRAINY SKIPPER

Every club has an intellectual. He sits at the bar, mind like a steel trap. He knows everything and has been everywhere.

It's pretty intimidating, until you actually sail with him. Only then do you realise that Old Mike, who left school at 16 and still can't spell yacht, is streets ahead when it actually comes to sailing.

Peregrene has a double first from Oxford and inevitably takes the intellectual approach to any problem. Old Mike's methods are more seat-of-the-pants, as shown in the evolutions below.

DOCKING IN A TIGHT MARINA

Peregrene uses his impressive grey-matter to construct a wind/tide vector, factors in the propwalk, considers the insurance position, crew dynamics and distance from the marina services. Meanwhile the boat ricochets off the harbour wall, rips off a Beneteau's pushpit and comes to rest with the bow deep in the side of a Bavaria.

Further down the marina Old Mike organises his crew and calls the marina office for someone to take the lines as he glides in.

ENTERING HARBOUR

Peregrene checks the chart carefully and notices a wreck in the western entrance. Despite the light winds and sluicing cross-tide he insists on going for the eastern entrance, adding nearly two hours to the trip and losing the last of his credibility with the crew.

Old Mike also scans the chart but notices the wreck has more than sixty metres of water over it, sails through the western entrance and is in the Café du Port well before closing time.

DEALING WITH A GAS LEAK

Peregrene smells gas and calculates that the butane molecule is heavier than the weighed average of the oxygen, nitrogen and carbon dioxide molecules present in air. Thus the gas must be lurking in the bilge. He instructs the crew how to bail out the space below the floorboards. The other crews in the anchorage are amused to see a chain gang of grown men passing apparently empty buckets along the line to be up-ended over the side, spurred on by their anxious skipper.

Old Mike's gas system leaks like a sieve. He turns off the stopcock and leaves the hatches open while the crew row ashore for supper.

ACID IN THE BILGE

Some orange juice is spilt during lunch and finds its way below. Peregrene has a steel hull; he calculates the pH of the juice and deduces that the acid in it will eat through the bottom. He immediately orders the crew to flood the bilge with fresh water, then bail out the (dilute) acid solution. This empties the water tanks, necessitating a long sail to the nearest marina.

Old Mike sprinkles some baking soda in the bilge, then sponges it out.

ONE MORE EXAM

Peregrene has never failed an exam in his life so is fully prepared for his skipper's test. He has crib sheets secreted about his oilies, mnemonics for variation and deviation and 17 ways of recovering a Man Overboard.

When the examiner fails him an almighty argument breaks out. Peregrene maintains that at neaps there is ample room under the power cable, but has been looking at the wrong month in the tables. In fact today is extra-springs and it will take a while before electricity is restored to Bristol.

Old Mike takes one look at the cable and turns back downstream. Paper qualifications are of no interest to him.

CHECKING THE WEATHER

Peregrene checks the forecasts on TV, in the newspapers and on several websites. He listens to the VHF, chats to the harbourmaster and draws weather maps for the next three days, which he confirms with a phone call to the Met Office. He finally concludes that it's going to be windy, so cancels the trip.

Old Mike opens the hatch, sniffs the air and goes back to sleep.

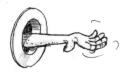

MOORING UP

Peregrene is chatting up an old girlfriend at the dock. 'So lovely to see you Samantha, last time must have been when you were at Girton and I was at Trinity. Golly, we nearly got sent down, do you rememb ...'

He breaks off as his yacht drifts slowly away; in his enthusiasm to be congenial no one has moored her securely.

Old Mike hooks on his permanent mooring lines and slouches off to the Mercator and Mizzen for a pint and a chat with the buxom barmaid.

Final score: Cranium 0, Seat-of-the-Pants 7

SOMEONE WHO SMELLS NICE ON BOARD

Picture the scene. A couple in a dinghy, about to land at a busy hard on a Sunday afternoon. Husband at the tiller, wife at the bow with the painter. Husband (in dictatorial and loud voice): 'Right, darling, when I say "jump" leap into the shallow water and pull us in. Ready ... Jump!'

The crowd hushes, she obediently springs off the bow ... and disappears under three metres of water. General mirth from the crowd, tight lipped control from the wife. Moral: know your depths, or your marriage will soon be plumbing them.

I once sailed with a couple who liked to argue. One evening I retired to my bunk while they went out to dinner and, sure enough, there was a big row between them in the restaurant. Eventually the man paid the bill and stalked off alone, back to the boat.

He chatted to me while cleaning his teeth, then hit the sack. At three in the morning the wife staggered back on board, in tears. She didn't know the name of our boat, in fact she didn't know much about boats at all. There were probably a hundred yachts in the marina that night and she had been on most of them trying to find us. I rolled onto my front as she described which bits of her husband's anatomy she was going to cut off first...

I woke the next morning to breakfast being prepared in the galley and reached for my hard hat. Not needed, as it turned out. 'Toast darling?', 'Thanks darling, pass the cafetiere my angel.' 'More champagne?' 'Super ...'

Amazing. How do men manage to turn these situations round? And why do otherwise sane women put up with this sort of treatment on a boat, and come back for more next weekend?

So it may be helpful to give some advice to those unlucky enough to be trapped on board with a bunch of Neanderthal males:

- Insist on getting off every night and staying at a local hotel. Lock your door, and in the morning refuse to let the crew share your buffet breakfast.
- In the marina, flirt with the guys on the next boat. With a bit of luck they will invite you over for a drink, at worst they will tell you how to get to the station. You escape either way.
- Ask if you can invite a friend. Say that she is blonde and leggy, which will guarantee a 'yes', but invite your dumpy friend Maud. Now you have an ally, will only be shouted at half the time, and will look slim in comparison. Maud, not having been so close to half a dozen men for years, will be delighted and may even finish up married if she really can produce a pavlova while heeled at 45 degrees in the middle of the night.
- Instigate a Foul Mouth Award and present it each evening.

- If the skipper is being really impossible, dive over the side and swim ashore.

However, in the early stages, it may pay to mind your P's and Q's. Here is a list of the top ten things NOT to say on a boat.

1. 'I'm afraid the loo doesn't work. It may be my Amazonian rainforest cleansing pads ...
2. 'Is my cabin en suite?
3. 'I'm afraid this little aerial thing broke off when I was getting over the rail ...
4. 'Surely it wasn't a problem discussing the recipe with Sarah on Channel 16 ...
5. 'When do you think the engine will go again? I need to get some eyeliner before the chemist shuts ...
6. 'I pulled out the little paddlewheel and got the weed off it. Now there seems to be a lot of water about ...
7. 'I've moved all the tools into the sitting room and hung my dresses in the locker. Hope that's alright ...
8. 'Could you come up? This ship is being really rude and hooting at us ...
9. 'The shower went cold after only 20 minutes ...
10. 'Don't be dramatic, it's only the rudder. Stop messing about and get us into the marina ...

If in doubt, pick off the crew one by one. For example, target the skipper and offer to help him with repairs. You will score valuable brownie points if you don your head torch and hold the spanner while the rest of the crew are drinking beer and reading yachting magazines.

Be obsequious to the navigator next. Tell him you really want to know how Cross Track Error works and ask intelligent questions about tidal heights. Try to stay awake while he gives you the answers.

In extremis, go on the foredeck and offer help with evolutions like pulling up the anchor (then you can retire to your bunk with a bad back) and gybing the spinnaker pole (lots of potential here for stretching your lycra swimsuit).

You will soon have them eating out of your hand. Then it will be you steering the dinghy ashore and them up to their necks in cold water as they pull you closer to the beach. Male chauvinism has never been a match for feminine guile. Lead your man to water but keep yourself out of the drink.

WHY ARE CREW BETTER THAN SKIPPERS?

When you're crewing it's natural to want to be the skipper. (In fact I've been on some boats where everyone thinks they ARE the skipper.)

But think about it for a minute. If you're crew:

- Your main concern in an emergency is packing your wallet, passport and a selection of chocolate bars.
- On the foredeck you can't hear orders. Just do it your way and let the blighters adapt.
- Anything breakable should have been stowed away – by the skipper, obviously. What's an expensive Chinese vase doing on a boat anyway?
- In fact, if anything breaks you don't have to fix it.
- Or pay for it.
- And best of all you don't have to unblock the heads, change the oil, find a sailmaker, organise the food or do the antifouling.
- Nor do you have to conduct crews' weddings, arrange their hospitalisation or bury them at sea. (If all three happen to the same person, tell the skipper to make Crew Selection more rigorous.)
- You can refuse to tack, gybe or anchor. From his 'position of authority' the skipper is helpless without you.
- You can say 'I don't understand spinnakers', then watch as the bag, blocks, guys, sheets, pole, uphaul, downhaul and halyard are prepared and the hoist completed. Then simply recline in its shade.
- You can treat a twisted spinnaker as an art form – only you have the time to appreciate the symmetry of an hourglass or marvel at the complexity of a double helix.
- And if it rips from head to foot, just call 'Next!'
- Work at being really useless. Then you get to steer a lot while the competent ones do all the heavy pulling and winding. Suckers!
- Errors can be fun! 'Sorry we hoisted the genoa upside down, skip. But good for a laugh, eh?'
- Your kitbag contains your personalised sweatband, aftershave/perfume, silk pyjamas and the latest summer reading. His contains WD 40, a new alternator, 30m of chain and replacement parts for the toilet.
- You can 'forget' to bring your laptop, mobile charger, towel, sleeping bag, money, insurance papers, wellies, etc. The Man In Charge is expected to sort it out.
- You can be allergic to copper (no antifouling), a vegetarian (no cooking), hopeless at maths (no navigating) and need 10 hours sleep (no night watches). It's the skipper's problem.

- At the end of the trip all you have to do is ... leave. It's the skipper's job to get the boat ready for next weekend.
- If you have a migraine you can go below for a few hours. Ditto if you want to send a few texts, listen to the cricket or chat up the good looking one who's off-watch.
- When the harbourmaster asks you to reverse into a tight berth in a howling crosswind you can hand over the helm, muttering 'Owner's prerogative, skip'.
- On arriving at a new port, step ashore and head straight for the bar. Remember, the skipper enjoys doing the paperwork at the Harbour Office. And while there he'll be delighted to ask about WiFi, check out the showers and get a few little essentials at the supermarket.

And what does the skipper get in return? He gets to pay for the boat, fits in with your holiday plans and has to be jolly with a splitting hangover.

Best to stay forward of the cockpit ...

THE CREW'S UNION

The Crew's Onion (as it is known) was founded in 1957 as a result of the notorious Hamble Riots, sparked by a lack of fresh vegetables on the yawl *Five A Day*.

MISSION STATEMENT
If passive resistance was good enough for Ghandi, it's good enough for us.

OBJECTIVES
- The Onion aims to regain power from those on Fantasy Island.
- A good crew intimidates the management by using all means legal, physical and psychological. Also by refusing to rub the skipper's back.
- In extremis, the Onion will back strike action, particularly if the boat is moored near licensed premises.

LIVERY
Members will wear Onion T-shirts for identification.
The front reads 'Support the Crew's Union' and the back: 'Strike a Skipper'.

Members will be blacklisted for wearing spoof T-shirts carrying the words 'Onion members are always pickled' or 'Strikers do it on a matchbox'.

ELIGIBILITY
We especially welcome members who are lawyers, brewers or who own dating agencies. Failing that, maybe you can supply waterproof mascara, have an auntie with a spare bedroom in Cowes or a database of skippers with large yachts?

BENEFITS OF MEMBERSHIP
- Our insurance will repatriate you if your skipper becomes too nauseous, garrulous or lecherous.
- Arbitration on arguments aboard. But do check first that you have done your share of steering, washing up, buying rounds and flattering the skipper.
- Voting rights to the annual Foulmouth Award. Count those four-letter words and your skipper could win an all-expenses-paid trip to Coventry and a lifetime's supply of mouthwash!
- 24/7 access to our No Win No Fee lawyers. Guaranteed to make the most authoritarian skipper mellow.
- Access to Onion publications:

  The great leap backwards: How to get off the foredeck and into the cockpit

The Dessication Diaries:
One man's quest to stay dry afloat. Comes with free pack of silica gel

One Out All Out:
The marine electrics manual

Sail Trim:
How to diet afloat

Mayday:
A guide to nautical emergencies and Morris dancing

Fuhrer on the Foredeck:
The blitzkrieg approach to sail handling

The Miser in the Cockpit:
A crew's guide to marine finance

The Skipper's Briefing:
101 tricky questions for you to ask. Includes complementary whoopee cushion

100 Skippers to Sail with Before You Die:
Finding the elusive ONE you can get on with

Join today and strike while the iron's hot!

PRETTY PROFILES

THE OFFICER OF THE DAY

The Miasma Creek Sailing Club insists that all its members do at least one duty per year, and it's Hugo's turn to be OOD this Sunday.

He arrives an hour before the start, as requested bringing two pints of milk for the galley and spare batteries for the hooter. A stopwatch is not needed since a benefactor donated an atomic clock, accurate to one second per century (a bit over the top actually, since most Miasma competitors are still on their moorings at the start gun).

The starter's box is to be his nerve centre for the day. It perches precariously on the end of the clubhouse like a tree house for adults, complete with steps made from driftwood supported by old Laser masts. The climb, though nerve-racking, affords a splendid view of the Miasma One Designs bobbing at their moorings: it's been a good week because only three have sunk.

Hugo's first job is to set the course. Acting on the principle that if this is done badly he may never be asked to do a duty again, he decides to create maximum chaos. This is to be achieved by a reaching start followed by a short leg to the first mark – a gybe round Sewage Outfall Buoy. Those left upright and untainted then head downwind across Sylvia's Shallows, a defunct oyster bed which has claimed numerous keels and rudders. The remainder of the fleet will then round Flash in the Pan, formerly a lightship but now a pancake restaurant, before heading back to the club line. Hugo designates 27 laps, on the principle that he can always shorten.

In the event the 'done badly' strategy exceeds even Hugo's wildest dreams. Not only will he certainly not be doing OOD again, he may even win the club's GBH (Greatest Boating Howler) award. Fifteen boats come to the line, but only ten leave it – the rest hard aground on the submerged Miasma One Designs. The Sewage buoy takes its normal toll, the capsized crews retiring for a tetanus jab, and Sylvia's oysters prove that you don't mess with out-of-date seafood. The last boat standing, Dr Bell's *Cirrhosis of the River*, crosses the line on lap 8 to thunderous applause from Doris (today's caterer), who is anxious that the Shepherd's Pie will spoil.

Luckily, Hugo has a chance to retrieve the situation in the afternoon race. This is a handicap pursuit, with the slowest boats starting first and the fastest last. The idea is that 90 minutes after the first start they should all be together, and the winner is the one ahead at that time.

The Miasma handicapping system is simplicity itself: the Optimists go off before lunch begins, the Mirrors go after the starter and the rest after the main course. Over the years this has led to some interesting tactics. One small Oppie sailor disconnected the Calor Gas cylinder before going afloat: by the time the fault was found and the food heated he was on the last beat. Another year the mother of one of the Mirrors produced a fantastic Beef Wellington and, most unsportingly, spotted dick and cheese and biscuits. Her daughter had finished before most of the competition had even cast off. The race was won last year by a crew of vegetarians who were legitimately able to decline the prawn cocktail and hamburgers, down a microwaved lasagne, and hit the course before the slow boats had reached the first mark. They have been referred to as the Veggie Burghermasters ever since.

This afternoon Hugo's culinary luck holds. Doris' garlic mushrooms are sufficiently numerous for the Optimists to get a reasonable lead, and the second helpings of Shepherd's Pie allow the Mirrors to get away.

At the 80 minute mark it's anyone's race. Hugo is positioned in the rescue boat, keeping station like a rugby referee monitoring a pushover try. The Optimists are pumping on every wave, the Mirrors are dodging the adverse current and the Miasmas are trying to blanket them all with their spinnakers. But as the finish looms the OOD's nautical luck runs out. Hugo stands up to get a better view at the same time as his helmsman stands to avoid a wave landing in his lap. The rescue boat capsizes, the atomic clock sinks – tragically early in its half-life – and the race ends in chaos, with many boats, some of which weren't even sailing, claiming victory.

With all the boats packed up, Hugo can only expect to reap the competitors' wrath. As they chuck him off the jetty he reflects that he has done his duty this day in a way that even Nelson couldn't have imagined.

THE RACER CHASER

Sarah has blond hair in a ponytail, blue eyes and a permanent tan. She arrives on board with her own oilies, harness and lifejacket and goes straight below to stow her gear. This includes half a dozen T-shirts emblazoned with messages for every eventuality:

Winch wenches do it in turns
Luff 'em and leave 'em
Let the guys take the strain
Happiness is a smooth bottom
Eat my wake

She comes on deck wearing her favourite: 'Grow your own dope' on the front, '... Plant a skipper' on the back.

This doesn't seem to phase her boyfriend Wayne, a Californian grinder who reckons winding in the genoa with an American accent is worth at least half a knot. Wayne was selected after exhaustive trials in the Cowes Week beer tent, and clinched the deal by climbing up the forestay then down the backstay, unblocking the heads and drinking ten pints of lager. This more than saw off the nearest competition.

Before leaving home Sarah downloaded the Sailing Instructions from the internet and laminated them, uploaded all the buoys as waypoints into her handheld GPS, and marked up the chart with no-go areas. This ensured her appointment as Navigator on arrival.

Her racing day begins with Pilates on the foredeck, followed by preparations for the crew's lunch ('Meals on Keels' as she styles it). When the skipper arrives she is in position at the nav station listening to the committee on Channel 37, giving no indication that three hours before she was still in the disco. From the forward cabin Wayne's snoring confirms that he too had a long night.

On the first beat Sarah tucks behind Wayne on the rail, ostensibly to keep the GPS dry but in fact to prevent her mascara running. She tucks the hood carefully into her anorak because once, cross channel, the person next to her was sick into her hood and the emptying procedure set off the whole crew.

Downwind, Sarah serves lunch: curry for ten on the rail, complete with poppadoms and chutney. This earns her three proposals of marriage and a job interview at the helmsman's pub, The Promiscuous Pintle. She tops off the run by nipping below to wash up, simultaneously packing the spinnaker and giving a bearing to the finish.

Having an attractive blonde on board can be a race winner. Heading for the line neck-and-neck, Sarah peels off her waterproof jacket and mid-layer to reveal a pink micro-bikini. The competition's onward charge falters, spinnakers flapping and telltales unwatched. As the winning gun fires, Sarah bows and descends below – before the goosepimples become too obvious.

A BIT OF A PEANUT
(Peanut Butter = nutter)

Reg, the backbone of our crew, runs a whelk stall in
the East End. He's actually a Pearly King, which
may explain why he leads us closer to the Pearly
Gates each weekend. Lovely chap, but hard to
understand. Take last Saturday, for example:

'Phew. That was a bit of a Rotten Row (1).
Bleedin' Frog (2) nearly hit the Salford Docks
(3). Terrible Sentimental (4) below, and Uncle
Willy (5) on deck. Reckon you lot could do with a Steffi
(6) and a Henley (7) at the Rub-a dub-dub (8). It's
on me, smart casual – well, wear Peppermint Rocks (9).

'Here's the Cain and Able (10). Take a Boiled (11).
Cheese grater (12)! Let's have some River Ouze (13).
Four bottles of yer best Rise and Shine (14) please.

'Here we go. Big Ears (15)! Right, we'll have two
Princess Di's (16) and two Richard Todds (17) with Zolas
(18) and Uncle Fred (19).

'Well, this is Tom and Jerry (20). Cheese (12), let's have the Rhubarb Pill (21).

'Looks OK. Rogan (22) or Pain in the neck (23)? No prob, keep the change.

'Phew, I'm Santa's (24). We'd better get back to the Frog (2) and that Peanut
the skipper before I'm Tom (25). Let's go!'

Those without a slang dictionary on board might like to borrow ours:

1. Rotten Row = blow	14. Rise and Shine = wine
2. Frog and Stoat = boat	15. Big Ears = cheers!
3. Salford Docks = rocks	16. Princess Di = pie
4. Sentimental Song = pong	17. Richard Todd = cod
5. Uncle Willy = chilly	18. Zola Budds = spuds
6. Steffi Graff = laugh	19. Uncle Fred = bread
7. Henley Regatta = natter	20. Tom and Jerry = merry
8. Rub-a-dub-dub = club	21. Rhubarb Pill = bill
9. Peppermint Rocks = socks	22. Rogan josh = dosh
10. Cain and Able = table	23. Pain in the neck = cheque
11. Boiled Sweet = seat	24. Santa's Grotto = blotto
12. Cheese Grater = waiter	25. Tom and Dick = sick
13. River Ouze = booze	

There's a dreadful rumour that we're also having a Glaswegian and a
Geordie aboard next weekend ...

THE BOWMAN

Sid has inherited the job of bowman on *The Ku Klux Clam* from his father, who also never won a race.

He keeps it because it's a slot no-one else wants, being cold and wet and well away from the galley. The plus side is that once forward of the mast the bowman is really in charge. If Sid hoists the spinnaker the skipper has little option but to bear away, and if he drops the genoa there's nothing for it but to motor back home.

An abundance of beer and stale pork pies has bulked Sid up to the size of a small dirigible. He can break out the anchor by moving aft, expose the rudder for repair by moving forward and fan the boat along in flat calm by moving from side to side. When Sid leans against the mast the leeward shrouds can be tightened by hand, and easing him overboard usually refloats the boat when aground. Most importantly, hiding Sid below while the boat was measured has given her a wonderful rating. The only negatives are that the waterline has had to be painted two inches higher, the fridge capacity increased and a special set of oilskins made by a marquee company.

Sid also has an inexhaustible supply of jokes. An example will give the flavour of spending a long night watch with him:

Three skippers are attending a friend's funeral. The poor chap had gone down with his boat after a collision with a tanker, and there were many kind speeches about what a good skipper he'd been.

At the wake, one of the friends asked the others what they would like to hear their crew saying if they had just gone down with their yachts.

The first, Lee King, said that he'd like to hear the crew say that he'd been a generous skipper, who always stood his round and organised memorable runs ashore.

The second, Portland Bill, said he'd like to hear that his navigation was spot on and his boat handling was perfection.

The third, Ben Dover, said 'Me? As I went down with the boat? I'd like to hear someone shouting 'Thank goodness! I can hear his lifejacket inflating'.

Like Sarah, Sid has a good collection of T-shirts. His favourite has on the front 'Beware of the skipper' and on the back 'The crew aren't trustworthy either'. Others include 'At sea, no one can hear you scream' and 'We like terra firma. The more firma, the less terror'.

You can now see the size of the problem. But, since the only remedy is doing foredeck yourself, you can understand why Sid has lasted as long as he has.

THINGS YOU'LL NEVER HEAR THE CREW SAY

- Nice work, skipper!
- Phew, without your experience that could have been so much worse ...
- You certainly know your COLREGS. A strobe light over two reds plus anchor lights making continuous sounds does mean a disco vessel aground.
- Can I hold the torch and umbrella while you fix all the leaks?
- No need to sail any closer, we can easily get to the airport from here. If we start at 2am and go via donkey, camel, rickshaw and gondola we'll be in good time for the 1900 flight.
- You relax with a beer while we go and pay the mooring fee.
- Bit of a mix-up with the swimsuits. Do you mind if we go topless?
- We've polished the mast, swung the compass, knitted a Somali courtesy flag and fumigated the bilge. Anything else before we buy you dinner ashore?
- We promise not to touch anything, and keep our mouths shut.
- No need for new sails, it's our trimming that's the problem.

- Although re-styling the keel and ripping out the internal furniture would give some more speed, we think daily circuit training for the six winter months will be more effective.
- We know how expensive it is to run a yacht so we're putting our Winter Fuel Allowances in the kitty.
- It looks cold at the wheel. Would it help if Samantha sat on your knee?
- Anyone can navigate to the wrong country. A holiday in The New Siberian Islands will be so much fun.
- The engine's dead and there's no wind? Great, we were secretly hoping for another night at sea.
- To have broken a strong fitting like this your crew must have the brains of a goldfish and the finesse of a rutting rhino.

THE FIRST PC CRUISE

We need to send a clear signal that crews everywhere resent being exploited for the transportational needs of their skippers. We plan to endow a chair in Crew's Studies specialising in linear, yachtinista-style thought. Students will experience cooperation and equality, while having their basic rights protected, i.e. a dry bunk and full access to the booze locker.

Crewed by these politically-aware professionals, a log of the annual cruise might make more democratic reading:

Cruise from the Peoples' Republic of Portsmouth to the Socialist Democracy of Salcombe.

EMPOWERMENT SEMINAR (formerly the Skipper's Briefing)

1. The interim skipper welcomed us aboard *Quango*, an equal-opportunity vessel.
2. A Facilitator (formerly, skipper) was elected. A Steering Committee was set up to choose the helms-people (now termed Directional Technicians). Jobs for the other co-workers were discussed. It was agreed posts should be awarded on merit, not closeness to some unobtainable ideal of appearance.
3. The previous skipper's carbon footprint was scrutinised, particularly the time when he stepped on a piece of burnt toast.
4. The fragrance-enhancement of the heads was welcomed, and its nasally-impaired status revoked.
5. The abuse of alcohol on arrival was discussed and adopted enthusiastically.
6. The one-destination policy enabled Salcombe to be chosen.

THE BOAT-SHARING EXPERIENCE (formerly, Passage Notes)

1000   Finish with engines. Boat sailing and harmonised with the environment.
1200   Quantitative Easing of Genoa. Speed increases to 6 knots.
1400   Fed up with incessant calls, Abby smashes Steve's mobile with her shoe. This is referred to as the Phone Whacking Sandal.

1500   Sam is seasick. To prevent marginalisation, his co-matelots adopt a food-abstention policy.

1700   John is waterproof-impaired when Abby borrows his oilies. He accuses her of cross-dressing and also nicking his towel. The issue is resolved using Cognitive Behaviour Therapy and by Steve telling John not to be a muppet.

1800   Saloon thermally enhanced by the ignition of precious fossil fuels (we light the cooker). A nutritious salt-free vitamin-enhanced meal is prepared. Co-workers dump meal over the side and heat pizzas in the oven.

2130   Voyage chronologically accomplished as the co-dependents arrive in the snug of The Freeboard and Lodging, with time for a nightcap at the Swiggit and Overfall.

FOOTNOTE
No sailors were harmed in the preparation of this log.

CAN YOU GET ON IF YOU'RE GETTING ON?

Sophie's first trip on the boat did not begin well. Reaching from the dock to put her handbag on the foredeck, she put pressure on the guardrail. The bow rope was a bit slack, and the boat moved seawards a couple of feet. Sadly, Sophie also moved seawards, and for a moment all we could see were a couple of her feet, and then not even that. I suppose the only positive aspect was the wet T-shirt effect as she clambered out onto the pontoon. Guys appeared from everywhere to offer a hand. Proving that sailors are real gentlemen.

Having said that, getting on and off is not always easy, especially for those getting on a bit. I remember sailing with the owner of a new 60-footer and taking him for a run ashore one night in Cherbourg. Slightly the worse for wear, we assisted each other back to the pontoon and thence to the boat. We were greeted by the towering black side of the yacht – the crew having forgotten to put out the steps. The owner tried to pull himself up on the stanchion, to no avail, muttering 'Bloody hell, I've been working all my life for a boat this big and now I've got one I can't get on it.' You had to sympathise.

Another elderly acquaintance, rowing drunkenly out to his anchored yacht late one night, was delighted to find his thoughtful crew had left a rope hanging over the stern so he could pull himself aboard. Gratefully heaving himself up, he was surprised by a huge bang followed by a heavy weight landing on him, capsizing the dinghy and pitching him into the oggin. It turned out the rope had been the automatic launcher for the liferaft, which had inflated with the speed of an airbag and thrust itself over the transom. The rest of the crew were sound asleep below, and were surprised to find the liferaft gently bobbing astern in the morning.

Nor have I escaped these problems myself. One summer, *Dancer* was moored in the Med bows-to the pontoon. Nursing a damaged toe, I was a bit concerned about jumping off onto the dock. My solution was to try squatting down first, lowering my weight to reduce the pain on landing. This was a mistake. My backside locked into the pulpit, forming a perfect pivot as I pushed off. My body rotated until my docksiders were pointing at the sun, then I slipped gracefully into the harbour head-first.

It's not all Bling, Bentleys and Barbados for these types and The Age Concern Sailing Team should think ahead. Install whatever is needed to get yourself aboard or ashore, be it derrick, crane or pogo stick. And if that doesn't work, go for a smaller boat.

HEALTH – A DOCTOR WRITES

Unfortunately we couldn't read his writing. Instead, here are the skipper's ideas on keeping the crew healthy.

1. Always have at least one nurse aboard, preferably in uniform. Failing that, an undertaker is often handy.
2. Clear out your home medicine cupboard into a box marked First Aid. (Stock up at home with stuff that's in date.) Transfer the box to the boat and site it at the back of the stern locker.
3. Ask the crew if they have any medical problems you should know about. Do this at the Skipper's Briefing: no-one will own up in public, and you get a tick on the checklist.
4. A pre-season boot camp will improve strength and flexibility. But with the crew starting at the fitness level of a lugworm, make sure you have a crash box ready. Plus the nurse/undertaker from Point 1.

On the other hand, the crew's medical ideas involve:

A. Sid's Patent Beer Cure for dehydration.
B. Staying out all night with Jim (to cure insomnia).
C. Pete's healthy victualling, which involves a different pie for each meal (followed by a varied choice of pastries).
D. Recognising symptoms: blood requires more tape on the split-pins, horizontality suggests new deckshoes, vomiting implies you need a new dishcloth (or better jokes).

Someone has to be ship's medical officer and if it's you, you need to be able to bluff. The sections below show how to handle most shipboard ailments.

SCURVY
Tell the sufferer that naval surgeon James Lind cracked the problem of Scorbutus (presumably a diminutive of sore butt) in 1875 by giving his crew citrus fruit. If your lads refuse anything that healthy, at least insist on lemon in their G&Ts and oranges in their Xmas stockings. Remind them that Five-A-Day does not refer to Blondes, and chips don't count as a vegetable.

SEASICKNESS
On a boat the brain can receive conflicting messages from your eyes, ears and muscles. These make you sick. (This is similar to the skipper's conflicting messages like 'Starboard side to, no port side to, maybe we should come in stern-first, actually I think bow-to would be safer for the rudder, sorry let's anchor while I make up my mind – no, the kedge you idiot ...' These also make you sick.)

Establish your credentials by mentioning that nausea is derived from the Greek word naus, meaning ship. (Of course, if they had any naus they wouldn't be vomiting on your ship in the first place!)

They will be hoping for a cure and a wristband is one answer. The pressure of its spike releases endorphins, which presumably then swim from side-to-side under the bow doing tricks, keeping the crews' minds off the problem. An alternative is seasickness tablets which work by making them too drowsy to be miserable. (On the minus side, the pills mean they can't operate heavy machinery like a washing-up pad or a deck broom.)

There are some good bargains to be had on a rough passage. One skipper I knew was so fed up with being ill that he gave the yacht to the crew in the middle of the night. Sadly for them the wind dropped at dawn, the sun came up promising a beautiful day, and he reneged on the offer.

CONSTIPATION

Most crews not only ignore their colons, they don't even use semi-colons! These are the types too lax to bring their laxatives: their vowels are bound to suffer. Of course, there's no real need for pills – a run ashore for a few pints and a vindaloo should do the trick. If not, get them to chew on some baggy-wrinkle for its high fibre content or consider a Mexican ENEMA (Eating Nachos Eradicates Most Afflictions).

SUNSTROKE

Overexposure to UV gives the crew sunburn. They probably looked pretty bad before, but now they are red and wrinkled as well. Get them to face north, say 'Aloe Vera' three times and slap on Davison's Patent Stubble Cream. If they're still ugly in the morning, a Botox clinic is the only answer.

DEHYDRATION

Seventy-five percent of the body's weight is water. (Otherwise there's no way you could pour yourself into those skintight jeans.) In the excitement of shouting at other crew members, sweating up halyards and generally breathing, people lose lots of water and start to wrinkle up (q.v. Sunstroke above). Symptoms include confusion, lethargy and irritability. This is probably the natural state of your crew so dehydration may go unnoticed. Permanent brain damage or death will give more of a clue.

Get the victim to drink small amounts of fluid often. If he is short on electrolytes get the correct stuff from the chemist. Drinking battery acid will seldom be effective.

To prevent recurrence, always wear your Hydrate© T-shirt, with the logo:

Find a solution: Water a sailor

Finally, if you need more detailed help, email A Doctor on one of these websites:

rhinohorn@fiverashot.org   quack@haventaclue.gov
wheran@on.it   scurvy@orange.net

If you can't get a reply, try:
www.amateur-amputation.org/hacksaw

And in extremis:
www.cheapfunerals.com/concrete/overcoat

BAA BAA SLACK SHEET ...

Sailors are just overgrown children, so it's not surprising they have their own nursery rhymes.

For example, here's Dr Foster reporting a match race between two three-man keelboats.

'Welcome to Radio Gloucester Live. This heat sees The Three Blind Mice racing The Three Little Pigs. The Pigs helmsman, Margery Daw, is see-sawing away at the tiller holding the Mice above the line, here's the countdown and ... Ding Dong Bell – they're off!

Heading up the beat the Pigs cover is merciless. Now the Mice are putting Humpty on the weather rail. He's egging them on and, with his extra weight... they're through!

At the top of the beat Contrary Mary, Mice's skipper, drops the tiller and hits the weather mark. The judges hoot and raise a flag, indicating a penalty. The delighted Pigs give her the rough edge of their tusks:

Mary had a little horn
In fog she set it honking
Then retreated down below
For some extra-curricular ... navigation practice

Now Daw and Mary swap gybes till the end of the run, when the Mice fail to give water. This earns them a Whittington (they have to Turn Again), plus further nastiness from the Pigs:

> I wish I was a fairy queen
> My rig all made of cotton
> I'd pull myself right up the mast
> And slide down on my ... head

Now they're on the final beat and the Pigs, determined to promote their sponsor, Wolf the Bacon, fire up their primus. This is a mistake. A sheet of flame ignites the mainsail and the Pigs get their buns very hot and cross. They limp home under jib alone, dragging their sail behind them.

Foster interviews them as they step off onto the *Hickory Dock.*

'Margery, how did it feel to have your lead snatched away?'
'Well, Doc, it was like a fairy story for the first half but then the lads literally got on their cock-horse to Banbury Cross.
'Paradoxically, this was probably a good moment for the Mice?'
'Yes. They anticipated what was going to happen before it even happened. After that we either suffered from apathy or we just didn't care any more. Now we're gutted – you know, matches don't come any bigger than these quarter finals.'
'Luckily, you've tasted the other side of the coin on so many occasions. Anyway, thanks Margery and congratulations on being Doctor Foster's Shower of the Match.'
'Thanks, Doc. I guess it's all about the two S's – speed and winning. Anyway, we haven't not given up hope that we won't be in the final next year.'
Well, for the Pigs right now there are more questions than answers being asked. This is Dr Foster returning you to the Middle Puddle Studio in Gloucester.

URANUS ON THE FOREDECK

Sonar Sam ('The Transducer') gives this week's nautical horoscope.

Author's Note: It is true that Sam's cosmic qualifications consist of reading Know the Game: The Night Sky, and a spell on the National Lottery. Similarly, his nautical expertise comes from one afternoon's sailing a model yacht on Kensington Round Pond. Nonetheless, his predictions are eagerly awaited by the yachting fraternity, and many dodgy yachts have been bought and many incompatible crews assembled as a result of his advice.

ARIES (MARCH 21–APRIL 20)
With Jupiter in conjunction with Mars, stick to tried and tested methods of getting things done. Keelhauling is useful, but remember you will need live crew for the return voyage. Aries can be deep thinkers, so night watches are a good time to solve some of life's great mysteries, e.g. 'If all is not lost, where is it?'

CANCER (JUNE 22–JULY 23)
You're beginning to look at life from a different angle, and are learning to handle other's criticisms. Tell them the boat will be afloat again at high tide and Jeremy was the idiot on the helm. The Sun's eclipse on Thursday will give an opportunity to try the nav lights.

GEMINI (MAY 22–JUNE 21)
Take maximum advantage of the luck coming your way. Thursday is particularly propitious. Lucky bearing: towards the bar. Lucky underwear: non-slip. Lucky exam result: topmark. Lucky crew: Lee Helm. Lucky number: 1.87 (if your draft is 1.86).

VIRGO (AUG 24–SEPT 23)
In the sailing world there are very few Virgos left. Styled as 'Nit-picking worryworts', they can be problematic in a crew and are best left to sail singlehanded. Famous Virgos include Robinson Crusoe, The Flying Dutchman and Jane.

Here are some of Jane's positive and negative characteristics:

Positive
Sympathetic – prepared to hold the bucket while you're sick
Organised – remembers to disconnect the shorepower before setting off
Witty and charming – only complains for 20 minutes when you run the boat aground

Negative
Perfectionist – wants ALL the old antifouling scraped off before applying new, even with the boat on piles and the tide rising
Self-disciplined – allows you to do the scraping
Good at detail – notices when you miss a bit

Finally, Sonar Sam's predictions for the year ahead.

The Fastnet will be deemed too tough so a new course will be devised from Cowes, round the Nab tower and back ... with 124 laps.

Russia will enter the market with a range of Cossack yachts. These come with an icebreaker bow and bulletproof sprayhood as standard, and feature the 'just one more revolution' furling system. A sister company is producing motor boats, the biggest of which, The Oligarch, is refuelled from its own Alaskan pipeline.

The America's Cup will be sailed in trimarans with foils, which only have a draught of 10cm. Wembley Stadium will be flooded for the regatta. Mexican Waves will generate the wind, boats will take their turns for a penalty (!) and spotting headers will become a national pastime.

BEAUFORT'S SCALES

Most skippers strut and swagger and generally behave like a *grande fromage*. If you're cheesed off with yours, try recounting the life of Sir Francis Beaufort (1774 to 1857). That should deflate his ego a bit.

Beaufort was shipwrecked at 15 due to a faulty chart, and devoted his life to improving matters. En route he invented contour lines, the Beaufort Scale for wind strength and weather notation for charts. He was a fellow of the Royal Society and consulted on many scientific developments. He administered the Greenwich Observatory, founded the Royal Geographic Society and promoted the development of Tide Tables. When Robert Fitzroy asked for a scientist to accompany him on the Beagle, Beaufort found him Charles Darwin. Beaufort ended up knighted, an admiral and Hydrographer of the Navy, which he turned into the finest charting institution in the world. Not bad for an uneducated lad who went to sea at 13.

But what if Beaufort hadn't been a polymath but a numbskull skipper like your own? His wind scale, still observation-based, might have looked more like this ...

Force	Windspeed (knots)	What the crew wear	Drink (effect on crew)	Food	Effect of drink on Skipper
0	0	Thongs	Beer (calm)	Pepper steak and tiramisu to follow	Hasn't the foggiest
2	4–6	Bikinis	White wine (eyes glassy)	Stew, on plate	Cold front
4	11–16	Shorts	Champagne (ripples of laughter)	Stew, in mug	Approaching trough
5	17–21	Oilskins	Red wine (Mexican waves)	Stew, overboard	Filling slowly
6	22–27	EPIRBs & airline neck cushions	Whisky (progress seriously impeded)	Stewgeron	Warm front
7	28–33	Exposure suits and prayer mats	Brandy (visibility affected)	Not really hungry, thanks	Becoming fresh
8	34–40	Wings and harps	Rum (crew see white horses and pink elephants)	Pass the bucket	Falling rather quickly

THE BLOG OF THE *BOYSTEROUS*

And now for something completely different! What follows is part of
the blog from the Oyster 53 *Boysterous* on her Atlantic crossing from the
Canaries to St Lucia. It was sent daily, by Iridium phone, to the ARC* race
organisers and also to friends and family.

It's included as an example of how the crew's composure can change on a
long passage. It begins sensibly enough, with details of weather, distance run
and so on. But gradually the sailors start to hallucinate: on Day 6 a young
Swedish underwear model is rescued, and is joined on Day 11 by a female
fitness fanatic. Meanwhile disaster strikes as the ship runs out of marmalade
but, undaunted, lavish preparations are in hand for the Mid-Atlantic Party ...

This blog is an example of how members of The Skippers' Club and The
Crew's Union *can* work together to get a small yacht across a large ocean.

DAY 1   SUNDAY 26 NOVEMBER – START DAY

Men and ships rot in harbour. We've had a great time in Gran Canaria but
now, with 700 litres of water and 75l of diesel – plus 67 litres of alcohol –
we're ready to go.

The start is a great spectacle with 230 boats in two divisions. We make
the best start in the Cruiser Division and put up the MPS (Multi Purpose
Spinnaker) only to be blanketed. There's only 10 knots of breeze so we
elect to motor for a magic 13 minutes to get clear of the pack. (We log our
motoring, and later incur a time penalty, but if we drop below 4 knots it's
probably worth it.) In clear air the MPS fills and we're off down the east
coast of Gran Canaria. 2,700 miles to go.

Abeam of the airport the wind strengthens and the kite becomes skittish.
After a couple of hours of flapping and wrapping it finally winds itself
round the forestay in a determined manner. Time to get it down, gybe
and pole out the genoa as a safer night rig. Colin puts in a waypoint at 20
deg N and 28 deg W, a mere 820 miles away. I suppose that is encouraging
– in a way. This target point will take us south (until the butter melts as
the sailors of old used to say) before we can turn west and head for the
Caribbean with the Trade Winds.

And then it all goes dark! Harnesses and lines on and start the watch
system – 3 hours on and 9 hours off with Colin 'floating' and doing the
cooking. He is also on call when things go wrong or big decisions are
needed. One such occurs on my watch – the wind has been veering all night
and, with our running rig, we are forced to deviate further and further from
our ideal course. Colin and I gybe the main and begin to head south west
again but elect to wait until daylight (and more crew on deck) before gybing
the pole. Shorthanded and in the dark these manoeuvres can take an hour
and the secret is manpower.

*Atlantic Rally for Cruisers

All night we run under genoa and main at between 5 and 7 knots and have clocked up 151 miles by noon the next day. A fine start!

DAY 2   27 NOVEMBER – GETTING INTO OUR STRIDE

We have been running with a goose-winged genoa (i.e. one sail each side) for 24 hours now and are pushing south fast. We did 156 miles yesterday, averaging 7.5 knots. Essentially, we are running parallel to Africa heading slightly west of the Cape Verde Islands. From email we have the weather grib files (wind arrows superimposed on the chart) and it looks best to continue on this course and gybe in the morning.

At night we had a near miss. The radar is a great help in spotting other boats and once it picks up a target you can ask the machine to track it. If the track goes through the middle of the rings on the screen you can either duck or take avoiding action. The whole process is made more interesting because we're doing 8 knots and can't change course much with the sails in the current configuration. In the event, the other boat passed a few hundred yards ahead, which is scary in the dark when it's hard to judge distance. Although we have 228 years of sailing experience between us, we are still learning from our mistakes.

Actually, we fit right in with the ARC profile. At the medical briefing the doctor explained how to stem the blood from a head wound by tying hair across it to hold the edges together. Then, looking round the room she corrected herself ... 'probably not enough hair here to make that work'. She looked like a child.

DAY 3   28 NOVEMBER – TRADE WIND SAILING AT LAST

We gybed onto starboard mid-morning as planned and spent a fabulous morning running in bright sunshine. This is what we came for – champagne sailing in the Trade Winds. We're bowling along at 8 knots on 259 degrees True. By a happy quirk of fate St Lucia bears 263. At this stage it's irrelevant but it feels good nonetheless to be pointing for home.

Occasionally we see another ARC boat but very rarely. It's amazing how 230 boats can disperse in 48 hours.

The first excitement this morning is running the watermaker. Start the generator, turn on the machine and Robert's your relation (or Bob's your uncle if you prefer). This little baby can make 40 litres an hour which should keep up with even our super-keen shower merchants.

Next up is David and his magic sextant. We learn how to pull the sun down to the horizon and the astro equivalent of the running fix. At the end of the exercise we are only eight miles out – not bad considering last time I tried I put the boat somewhere in the Sahara Desert.

The plan tonight is more of the same, but heading as far south as we can – the grib files are showing lighter winds ahead and we want to be in a position to reach rather than run through the light airs. Whether this strategy will work in practice is in the lap of the gods. *To be continued ...*

DAY 5 30 NOVEMBER – A STITCH IN TIME

The wind last night was very light. Eventually, at 2am, I called the skipper. On port gybe we were heading for the South Pole, on starboard for America. And in any case we were only doing 4 knots and Christmas would be over by the time we reached St Lucia. Like a sensible person he ordered the sails down and the iron topsail to be hoisted until we hit more breeze - in the event, after 62 miles of motoring.

The general idea is to sail when we can and motor to the next weather system when we can't. And no, we can't motor all the way because we only have fuel for 1000 miles (and also the time penalty would be horrific).

Today was spent trimming the spinnaker. David trimmed it in the morning and Paul and I trimmed it in the afternoon. The difference was David did his trimming on the saloon table: we'd managed to put a two metre rip in it and he patched and sewed for four hours, only stopping to staunch the blood. At this rate we will definitely run out of sticking plaster. (Actually, on the last Atlantic crossing he was strapped to the boom for 12 hours stitching the mainsail so, as we kept telling him, this rip is pure unashamed luxury.)

And so to that other vital domestic skill aboard – cooking. We are running a competition to name the *Boysterous* restaurant. Chi-chi ideas like 'Fleur de Sel' were floated but the front-runner is 'Colin's Caf'. Please let us have your entries by email. At the same time please give your answer to the eternal question, 'Why did the chicken cross the Atlantic?' I am sure you can improve on Paul's 'Because it had the wind behind'. And after so much education ...

Finally on the food front, the Week 1 supply chest has run out of marmalade and apparently there won't be more until Week 3. Is this a case of Jam Tomorrow?

You can see that the light winds are taking their toll of our sanity ...

DAY 6 1 DECEMBER – PARTY TIME

A slow sailing night and motoring all morning. At LAST the barometer is dropping, the sun is out with a vengeance and we are hoping we are past the ridge of high pressure and can put some miles under our keel. At the time of writing (6pm) it's 26 deg C and the sea is 29 deg C. Wind's up and we are running at 7 knots on 271 deg true. We have passed the 800 mile mark and are third in class. The guy who is second is 200 miles north so should have less wind than us. And we don't know how much motoring *Splendid* has done, but he'd better get his skates on over the next 2000 miles because we're after him.

Today is John's birthday. When he told us how old he is we threatened to cut off his leg and count the annual rings. But 73 isn't old these days.

First off was the Skipper's Brunch, with *Boysterous*'s own-label Champagne, a promiscuous little assemblage of Pinot Noir and Chardonnay, followed by scrambled egg on toast with bacon and tomato, plus fruit salad and yoghurt (anti-scurvy).

Next was to have been the noon swim, abandoned after David mistakenly told John that, in the water, he is not necessarily top of the food chain. (In fact the only predators we've been seeing are flying fish.)

Tea was a lavish affair with balloons, pannacotta, dolphin cups and plates and lots of jostling for position. Sadly no jelly, but plenty of balloons, compulsory hornpipes on deck winding up with a rendering of *Pomp and Circumstance*. Fantastic at full volume with the Atlantic all round.

Just when we thought the day's excitement was over, a liferaft was spotted ahead. When we pulled alongside we found only one occupant, Samantha, a former Miss Sweden finalist. Things on *Boysterous* may never be the same again.

And so to the current state of play on our competitions:

Why did the chicken cross the Atlantic?
1. Because he eggsagerated the distance (David)
2. To avoid Foul weather (Tim)
3. He confused Richard Matthews with Bernard Matthews (we didn't understand it either)

And the Boysterous *restaurant?*
1. The Tradewinds Diner
2. The Transatlantic Transport Café
3. Sloop John B

Finally, a little Janet and John story for John who is overexcited after the party:

Hello Janet
Hello John
Do you know how to sail?
John does
Here is John's yacht
Can you see the sails?
John often sails with Samantha
Can you see her lying on the foredeck?
John can
Now it's the end of the voyage
Can you see John's wife, securing the mooring line?
John can
Can you tie knots?
Samantha can.
John has been teaching her.
'Why were you so long coming in?' asks John's wife
'I was in the stern cabin with Samantha. She was getting ready to take her kit off. And I was showing her how to make a sheet bend,' says John.
Have you ever been hit with a winch handle?
John has
Poor John

DAY 8   3 DECEMBER – THOUGHT FOR THE DAY: IF THIS IS CHAMPAGNE SAILING, ARE WE COLIN'S GRAND CRU?

A fast night and day culminating in our best run so far – 191 miles. Not surprising in 18 – 25 knots of wind with 8 knots on the clock for hours at a time. Max speed 11.7 knots slithering down a massive wave.

Slight drama at 3am when the foreguy to the spinnaker pole snapped and all hell broke loose. Five guys on deck in record time and an hour's work to roll away the genoa, lead new lines and roll it out again. Sounds simple but not so easy on a heaving foredeck in the dark. Paul did fantastic work up front and the skipper awarded us all a Kit Kat from the naughty cupboard. Believe me, gentle reader, this signifies a major achievement.

We are having trouble on board with communication. Our skipper is inevitably in the thick of it on the foredeck but those upwind on Fantasy Island (i.e. in the cockpit) are having trouble hearing and/or understanding his commands. So I have been delegated to put together a *Boysterous* Dictionary.

Sheet!	pull in the sheet
Sheet!	let out the sheet
Sheet!	the sheet's caught
Sheet!	these waves are big!
Rhumb line	derivative of Rum Line, the reason we're on this trip in the first place
Source of fix	the second reason we're on this trip
Bearing up or down	depending on whether you're cheerful or giving birth
Distance run	obviously small, given the confines of a small boat
Heads	please put yours here while being sick
Stern cabin	where you're invited for a serious talk with the skipper (unless you're Samantha, when it becomes a companionway)
Heel	the blighter who stole my sunscreen
Ground wind	do we really need to go into that?
Apparent wind	ladies' version of the above
True wind	macho male version of the above
Navigator	navigators onboard never answer unless comments are prefaced by banter such as 'Ho, COG baby, how yo SOGging? Been on any good rhumb lines recently? Any chance of a reciprocal bearing after supper? No? Mind if I do? Eventually they will reveal where we are, where we're going and if you have time to fit in a Mars Bar
Skipper	a man who can ruin your lovelife in one report
Propeller	alternative method of getting Samantha into the stern cabin
Genoa	or did you just meet her at the crew party?

NOAA	weather reporting system, compatible with our electronics
ARC	boat to be compatible in
NOAA's ARC	a boat where you have to be compatible with a lot of animals – e.g. *Boysterous*
Deviation	not with five men on board
Variation	sadly, ditto
Naughty cupboard	store for Mars Bars etc., or place for carrying out deviation, variation (q.v.)
Great circle route	I wish I'd stayed at home. I could be on the tube now going to my cushy job
Wind	what you need before you can make any progress, as in 'wind and dined'
Ambient food	we still haven't worked that one out

1611 miles of this rubbish to go.

DAY 9   4 DECEMBER – 'SOMETHING BEGINNING WITH S'. A GUIDE TO THE MENTAL AND PHYSICAL HEALTH OF THE OFFSHORE CREW

Another stonking night and morning resulting in 192 miles on the clock and a maximum speed of 12.7 knots. It's getting warmer and the boat is rolling more which makes it harder to sleep. It's also annoying to have to hold onto everything on the table and on occasion to eat your dinner out of your lap. Shorts with sticky croutons are not much of a fashion statement really.

We have sorted out the ropes now and can gybe in 20 minutes - a distinct improvement on the hour it used to take. But we only need to gybe once a day now to keep near the middle of the track to St Lucia, which is in our sights. We should pass the halfway mark tonight.

This is reassuring even though we have enough medicine to keep the NHS going for a month. The Category C pack supplied was enhanced by John on a shopping trip in Gran Canaria with his sister, who speaks Spanish. Due to a slight misunderstanding, we now have suppositories for most common ailments, latex gloves (very useful for washing up), absolute alcohol (we have our eye on that) and a face mask (well, would you want to go mouth-to-mouth with any of these characters?). Needless to say, after one look at this lot and at the gleam in our First Aider's eye as he polishes his syringes, the crew are determined to stay healthy and the only medical equipment used has been a sticking plaster for a pricked finger, which promptly fell off (the plaster, not the finger). And the only medical advice, for a bruised palm, has been to hold a cold beer tightly. Not exactly the Royal College of Surgeons.

In ancient China, the system was that you only paid your doctor when you were healthy. John is proposing this system aboard, which would be fail-safe for him i.e. he either gets paid or gets to use his suppositories in anger. Needless to say we are resisting this. Poor John.

As the sun goes down the little yacht heads deeper into the Atlantic, a bone in her teeth as she tracks faultlessly through the foaming brine, her trusty crew looking forward to the beauty of the balmy night watches ... (author is carted off by men in white coats).

DAY 10 5 DECEMBER – 'ONE WORD IS WORTH A THOUSAND PICTURES'

We batted on through the night and most of today on starboard gybe at 8 knots in 20 knots of wind, putting on 190 miles for the 24 hour period. In the small hours we passed the halfway mark, which was celebrated by cracking open the final jar of jam at breakfast. One micron each. We know how to live.

Our only problem has been chafe: we have to pull in the mainsail to stop it rubbing on the spreaders and last night the spinnaker pole foreguy almost chafed through on the side of a block. At this rate we will run out of rope.

But our troubles are as nothing compared with *Compromise*, whose crew sent a Mayday asking for their skipper to be evacuated for medical reasons. The superyacht *Mirabella V* is standing by. *Mustang* was dismasted the day before and is now thankfully motorsailing towards St Lucia with a jury rig in place. *Nunki* hit a whale but sustained no damage, although the poor whale is taking industrial quantities of headache pills. Two other whales were seen in the vicinity.

We had hoped to send a selection of photos for our readers to caption. Unfortunately this involves too much memory for our Iridium phone to send, so instead we propose a reverse caption competition – we give you the captions and you imagine the photos.

Picture this:

'The liferaft doubled perfectly as a bouncy castle at the halfway party.'
'Samantha was having difficulty combining her dual roles of navigator and part-time brassiere model.'
'John finally agrees to give up the raindance and make water using the Seafresh Ocean 'A' Watermaker.'
'Colin perfects Back Passage Stew, a dish served on the second half of a journey and made with leftovers from the first half.'
'David demonstrates an interesting version of CPR on Samantha.'
'Paul's lifejacket inflates in the shower, showing the worth of a tight crutch-strap.'
'The skipper, retraining the toaster as a kettle.'
'David explains the difference between a great circle route and the rhumb line course using a pineapple and a waffle.'

Our other excitement has been filling in the ARC questionnaire on 'The Most Useful Gear On Board'. Presumably they are hoping for comments on watermakers, microwaves, chartplotters etc., but the crew would like to suggest the following:

1. Hull
2. Keel
3. Bolts for holding 1 to 2
4. Any suitable means of calling for help
5. Any suitable companion to pass the time until help arrives
6. Holiday brochures for next year's RELAXING BEACH holiday

Tomorrow, we are joined on board by Birgit, a 22 year old Scandinavian student who would like to travel and help people. Will this affect the exquisite timing and teamwork currently exhibited on *Boysterous*? Will the swede remain our favourite vegetable? Or, indeed, will Birgit's experience come in handy? Tune in to the next thrilling blog ...

DAY 11 6 DECEMBER – 'WE BUILT THIS COUNTRY ON ROCK AND ROLL'

Another good night and morning giving a noon-to-noon run of 211 miles and a maximum speed of 13.9 knots. We are still in third place in our class but closing on the second boat, who is some 60 miles ahead with 1033 miles to go. He will lose a bit on handicap too, because he is a faster boat. We are currently on port gybe heading straight down the rhumb line at between 7 and 10 knots. This is the way to travel!

On the disaster front we have heard on the email that *Why Not?* has sent out a Pan Pan because they have lost their steering and are currently drifting. This is everyone's nightmare: no-one relishes the prospect of hand steering for 1000 miles in this.

We ourselves have a nasty squeak from the wheel which we can't place. The autopilot is on sensitivity 9 out of 9 to help cope with the big waves rolling under us and is in constant motion. We are so aware of the contribution it is making that we launch a competition to give a name to the little beauty. Front runners are Lonely, Helmit, Buttons, and Merve (the Swerve), but my favourite is Pontius. We'll see.

More news on the competition front. We have entries from John Kingsley, stormbound in Norway, for the Naming Colin's Café award. Although Meals on Keels has merit we particularly like the subtle Heads, You Win.

We have a request to say more about what it's like out here (and presumably a lot less about what Samantha is up to).

The overriding factor is that none of the crew has ever been on a 3000 mile run before. Although a fast way to travel, the sails are edge-on and there's nothing to stop the boat rolling – for three weeks! Sleeping is problematic as it is difficult to form a working relationship with your bunk. The wide double bed that looks so attractive in harbour is lethal at sea where you need a narrow, high sided coffin that grips you on both sides. Duvets and pillows are used to wedge between the body and the leecloth to help kill movement. I am seriously thinking of tying myself to the bunk, but as a single man have no experience of this.

Would Sir like another roll?

Even simple activities like eating and washing up revolve around rolling. Anything left to itself slides off the table or work surface so, for example, to make a cup of tea your friend holds the electric kettle while it boils. Meanwhile you get out 5 cups and try to wedge them while you (or another friend) reach for the tea bags and milk. Once poured, you have a few seconds to distribute the cuppas to the crew before the whole lot finishes on the floor. Just a simple three-man job.

Once you've drunk your tea you wash your cup, dry it and put it away, because there's nowhere safe to put it down and Colin is rightly proprietorial about his bone china.

Moral: Keep the galley floor clean, as your dinner may have to be scraped off it one day.

And finally ... the arrival of Birgit

Shortly after the clocks had gone back, Birgit was transferred aboard from the Swedish maxi *Volvo Broom Broom*. This has done the crossing in a record 8 days, and was already on its way back to Europe. Due to the quick run, Birgit had only done 14 spinnaker peels, 23 gybes and eight dinners for the 18 young Vikings on board and felt cheated. She put in a request to ARC Control for 'some action at the cutting edge' – resulting in the transfer to *Boysterous* for the last 1000 miles.

The skipper gallantly offered to convert his fruit net into a makeshift hammock, leaving the double bunk below for Birgit. This was rejected on the grounds that Birgit would prefer to sleep on the windward rail for added leverage. When asked which job she would like on board she replied, 'On a small boat like this? All of them.' In the event she is given a wide brief - rather appropriate in her case - the 3-6 am watch, pumping the main on each wave, and converting distances run for each of the 230 boats into finishing times, allowing for their differing handicaps. We expect this to keep her quiet for the first 24 hours, freeing us professionals to get on with the serious business of yacht racing ...

DAY 12 7 DECEMBER

At about 8.30 last night we passed the psychologically important point of 1000 miles left to go. It's amazing how this trip has changed our perspectives: the 60 miles across the Channel to Cherbourg was normally something of a big deal but now 1000 miles is 'just' a sprint to the finish. And still on that comparison, the Channel is 60 metres deep whereas we have 4160 metres under our keel.

There were some light patches in the night so we 'only' managed 189 miles for the noon-to-noon run. We calculate we are lying about 20th overall, third in our class and are the top Oyster. But we're not counting any chickens, even though we have plenty of ideas why they crossed the Atlantic. As I write we've just gybed onto starboard and are hurtling down the rhumb line. It's a drag race now to St Lucia.

On the disaster front *Why Not?* has confirmed that she has lost her rudder, but is proceeding to St Lucia anyway. I seem to remember doing some rudderless sailing in RYA Level 2 in a dinghy on a pond, but 1200 miles in this sea is quite another matter. It will be a great feat of seamanship when they make it and we wish them all speed.

You look lovely in this damnable moonlight
I once asked Mike Golding what they did differently at night on *Group Four*, racing round the world. 'Nothing' was his reply. 'We do exactly the same as in the daytime.'

I have to report that, for us ordinary mortals, it's much harder at night. If you're going to be sick you're more likely to feel bad then, when you can't see the horizon. It's hard to set the sails when you can't see them. And you have to work out the risk of collision from your victim's lights (though I must admit we haven't seen a boat for over four days now). But at least you're on your own, the rest of the crew being in bed, so you finally get a bit of peace and quiet for three hours!

I've always hated sailing at night, but on a long passage it's probably the most enjoyable part. Last night the moon was out, the stars were shining and the Beatles were on my Walkman. The boat was fizzing down the waves at eight knots and my comrades were asleep down below marvelling at my skill in navigating them fast and safely to a new and exotic continent. (Some hope. They're clinging to their bunks willing you to keep the boat level for a few minutes so they can nod off.)

Hull of a day at the office, darling?
So what do we do all day? It's amazing, but there never seems enough time! Someone is always on deck, concentrating on sailing the boat (hopefully). Sometimes, we're all on deck, carrying out what the Navy call 'an evolution'. Then there's eating, sleeping, writing the blog, fixing things, making water (!), navigating, calculating how we're doing, communicating with the outside world, chatting, cooking, clearing up, and sleeping again. A full and varied life.

Meanwhile, back at the raunch ...
The lads are finding it difficult to adapt to having two women on board. The watermaker is running full time keeping up with the showering, the smell of aftershave is overwhelming and socks and underwear are drying on the rails where once only sheets and preventers plied their trade.

Our language, always suave, has reached new heights of erudition.
'Would you mind pulling in the sheet please, if you have a moment?'
'Certainly. Anything else while I'm down here?'

It didn't take long for Birgit to meet Samantha. They had once shared a flat in Stockholm when Samantha was modelling for Uplift International and Birgit was doing an MSc in Sport Science. Their opening exchange led us to suspect it might not have been a happy time.

BIRGIT: 'Samantha darleeng. Lovely to catch up. I see you've kept your beautiful figure, and added so much to it.'

SAMANTHA: 'Hi. Great. You're off course 10 degrees and the lazy sheet's chafing.'

Where will it all end? Will the crew be able to get into the heads in the morning?

Will the gimballed ironing board be a success? Will the Hoovering lessons pay off?

More tomorrow ...

DAY 13 8 DECEMBER – WHO YOU GONNA CALL? CHAFE BUSTERS!

Another great night and 204 miles to show for our efforts. As I write the CHAFE team (a subsidiary of SMERSH) are on deck clearing the night's crop of flying fish and trying to keep ropes and sails in one piece. One roll every 4 seconds for three weeks is ... nearly half a million rolls.

Two disasters on board. A jar of mustard and a jar of Rogan Josh went head to head in the fridge, presumably going for the hot slot of the yacht award, and spattered glass and seasoning over everything. Shortly afterwards a mug jumped off the draining board and splintered on the floor. My fault that one ... a case of mea cuppa.

In the fleet another boat, *Arnolf*, has lost her rudder. And a yacht, not connected with the ARC, has been dismasted and is proceeding to Barbados – without lights. That's an incentive to keep awake on the night watches.

The first boat is home! This is the Italian *Capricorno*, in a new record time. She is a 25 metre long maxi, and it must have been a wild ride. Congratzione guys.

We thank Shelley Baxter and John Kingsley (the inventor of Back Passage Stew) for their contributions to the competitions. We are also the Project for Year 6 of the Wych Primay School on Malvern, which is marvellous although I hope the teacher gives them the expurgated version.

Today's competition? Janet is having a tidy up below. Can you help her put the right object in the right person's cabin? (John can, but he knows that Paul sleeps on the top bunk and Samantha's cup size is D.)

Colin	Heart rate monitor
Samantha	Psion News
John	Abseiling harness
Tim	Silk dressing gown
Birgit	Two melons
Paul	Magnum of Chateau de Chateau '82
David	Health and Efficiency Annual 1987

And so to Crew's News

Colin has had to separate the girls, Samantha to Port Watch and Birgit to Starboard. If things get worse we may need a catamaran for the return trip so each can have her own hull. (Although Birgit is a bit of a dog, we think she might like a cat.) Otherwise things are much as always ... the aftershave epidemic has subsided after Samantha casually dropped details of her current boyfriend into the conversation. We understand Ungala plays second row for Western Samoa and is a Rhodes scholar at Oxford, on the brink of finding the lost moon of Uranus. Forget it lads ...

DAY 14 9 DECEMBER – LUCKY FOR SOME

We're entering an area of lighter winds (e.g. 12 knots) with vicious squalls (up to 46 knots this morning). This makes life difficult because we need full sail in the light but reefs and rolled up genoa in the heavy. No rest for the Grand Cru there.

Taking his rest last night, Paul was just finishing his book when a flying fish sailed through his open hatch and landed on him. The newest squid on the block was despatched with the edge of the book. And the title? *Fear of Flying? The Compleat Angler? Jaws? One flew into the Cuckoo's Nest? Cannery Row?* We leave you to decide.

It is a tradition on this boat to hold a Captain's Cocktail Party on the day before landfall. Your invitation is below and we look forward to welcoming you on board.

> The Captain and Crew of *Boysterous*
> request the pleasure of your company at
> THE CAPTAIN'S COCKTAIL PARTY
> to be held on board at 14 3.470N 59 22.394W
> at 12 noon on Monday 11 December.
>
> Dress: Ties will be worn
>
> RSVP

Hamming it up

The Cru believe the skipper has a pig in his cabin. We have had pork several times now, sometimes presented as chicken, sometimes as steak. Also, we cannot believe that the strange strangled grunts coming from Colin's cabin around midnight are human. We have a cunning plan:

1. To rename Colin's Caf 'The Trotteria'.
2. To give each dish a posh sounding name, thus taking the mind off the meat's origin e.g. Hams on horseback, Trotter a l'orange (Dell Boy's Delight).
3. To crack jokes about pork, e.g. Did you hear about the butcher who backed into a bacon slicer and got behind with his orders?
4. . To refer to the Cunningham as 'The Sly Pig', as American crews do.
5. To recite quietly, 'This little pig went to cockpit, this little pig stayed at boom, this little pig had first reef and this little pig went wee, wee, wee all the way to the heads.

Somehow, we think this approach may be too subtle to be effective.

The thin end of the wedge

The other excitement today was finding that the mast chocks were falling out. The mast goes through a hole in the deck and on down to sit in a shoe on top of the keel. There are wedges round the mast at deck level to stop it clanking around and destroying the deck. But with all the flexing and pounding the wedges were coming out and we had to reef to take the stress off so we could try to get them back in. With a combination of hammering from below and heaving from above, this has been successful and as a temporary measure, the chocks are tied in with a sail tie. Plus the creaking makes the boat sound like a rerun of Master and Commander (we always take the lesser of two weevils). Heaven knows what it will be like tonight when we are trying to get to sleep.

The good news is that we have so much diesel and hot water that the Skipper has decided that we could all do with a real shower, so don't let that put you off coming to the Captain's Cocktail Party. All the usual crowd will be there!

DAY 15 10 DECEMBER

There has been much discussion and criticism of this blog onboard and I have offered to present today's in a more professional form, being guided by the great diarists of the age. Here is how Samuel Pepys might have written it:

> Up early and to my mistress, Poled-out Jenny. She in the best of spirits, having passed the night merrily on the foredeck. We discourse most pleasantly and she makes several jibes about the plague and a little hot spot she knows in Pudding Lane. We dispute the relative levels of discomfort in 17th Century London and present day St Lucia. No conclusion is reached, so to Mistress Hall's Coffee House and a clay pipe or two ...

DAY 16 11 DECEMBER

After many days of having the Atlantic to ourselves it has become like Piccadilly Circus out here. This has re-awakened the competitive instincts of the crew and particularly the skipper, clearly not a man to give an inch on the racecourse. At four in the morning a yacht approached us on port gybe. Much flashing of torches on the sails persuaded her to bear away, and she sailed a parallel course for a couple of hours, then tried again to cross. In true Naval tradition the skipper refused to give way until, muttering things about 'Johnny foreigner', he reached up across the intruder's transom and pulled ahead, leaving her wallowing in our wake. As I write, two other yachts have appeared on the horizon. After nearly 3000 miles at sea, it's getting crowded.

Under the affluence

I am now able to report on the Captain's Cocktail Party, the embargo having been lifted when the deal with Hello! magazine fell through.

The party began 100 miles offshore and the skipper, resplendent in reefer, tie and long socks, welcomed each guest on deck to the strains of *Sloop John B*, our signature tune (the phrase 'This is the worst trip I've ever been on' sticks in the memory). The Cru had made a special effort, some even finding a clean shirt for the occasion and all wearing the compulsory tie (sorry, I don't think a harness line qualifies, old boy).

Samantha is fully decked out, sporting 'something she just threw on' but nearly missed. So revealing is the micro outfit that she catches the eye of Lotsa Luca, the Italian magnate (for women) and owner of the 120 foot powerboat *Grande Bananaaa*, which rendezvoused at the waypoint. After the party she jumps ship and disappears into Luca's stern cabin, the last we hear of her save some hair-raising reports in the tabloids.

Birgit has other ideas about how to gain attention. She announces that sailing *Boysterous* has not been the challenge she wanted, so intends to dive overboard and swim to the east coast of St Lucia, hack her way across the island with a machete, and be on the dock to take our lines when we come in. In the event, due to the large compass variation in this part of the world, she misses St Lucia and is beached on Martinique. There she falls in with the crew of the Spirit 54 that was used on the new Bond movie, and is hired as a stunt double for the next film.

It is thus, gentle reader, that we manage to finish with the same number of crew that we start with, an underlying principle of yacht racing.

Of all the bars in all the world ...
For the final run in we have a perfect afternoon: blazing sunshine, warm blue sea, Force 5 breeze and all sail set. Our plan is to manoeuvre round the north end of St Lucia, calling for water on any converging boats, nip south down the western shore and blast across the finish line in the early hours of the morning. See tomorrow's blog for the reality.

And finally, some late news – St Lucia police report that the thieves who stole the laxatives from John's First Aid kit are still on the run.

The lighthouse keeper at the north end of St Lucia has been arrested for flashing. He asked for 7 million other offences and one group flash to be taken into consideration.

While, at the southern end of the island, the lighthouse keeper has been accused of joining the occult. At the hearing our navigator was asked to leave the court for using course language.

And finally, the workman at the yard that put our spreader on upside-down has been diagnosed with rigger mortis.

So it's goodnight from me.

And it's goodnight from him, him, him and him.

DAY 17 12 DECEMBER
We finished today at one minute to midnight. The log read 2770 miles and it has taken us 15 days, 14 hours and 59 minutes. We are the 57th boat to arrive but we have no idea how we have done on handicap and of course there are still 173 boats to come in.

The main problem was finding the finish! It was a dark night and the lights of the town obscured the committee boat and buoy. And, ironically, there was a torrential downpour just for the two minutes that we were finishing (the only rain we've seen for three weeks). So we didn't get our finishing photo on the line and had to call up the organisers. 'Welcome to St Lucia! Strewth! The weather was great until you guys showed up' was his reply. At least we didn't have to wash the decks.

We had heard that the people here are welcoming but were bowled over by the constant hooting of horns and cheering as we motored up the harbour. (We later learned that there had been an election during the day and the winning party was celebrating!)

The ARC guys were on the dock to take our lines and give us each a rum punch, the first serious alcohol we have had for three weeks. Unfortunately, they also gave us the bottle.

I had mentioned to the Cru that the hardest part of a race for Ellen McArthur is the first step ashore, but our team seemed to have no such inhibitions and within 30 seconds of docking the party was in full swing.

Birgit is in luck, the next boat is Swedish and there are half a dozen blond guys on board. On the other side are the Irish, who have crossed with no more creature comforts than a bucket (actually, they had two but never found what the second one was for. Although, on reflection, it was probably The Ladies.). As a result of all this we finally hit our (level! wonderful!) bunks at 4am and slept (in some cases) until 2pm.

At last our Iridium phone is working again (we have borrowed a new modem from the Swedes) and it is great to have everyone's messages – particularly the replies to our Captain's Cocktail Party invitation. Most of the ladies wanted to know in advance what Samantha and Birgit would be wearing and how high killer heels Colin will allow on board. One asked for the life raft to be launched to give her a soft landing as she parachuted down. Several planned to wear bikinis and there was general concern at the cost of hiring private jets. In all a very enthusiastic response and next time we will give more notice and make sure it is in the Times Court Circular.

This afternoon we went to see *Mustang*. Beautiful boat but the mast certainly looked pretty sad – it had broken off just above the first spreader and they had to motor the last 1200 miles. Sadly the boat that lost its rudder was abandoned and the crew taken off, exhausted.

So now we are in the Caribbean! It's hot, the sea is 31 degrees, the reggae is pumping and there are happy smiles and welcomes all round. We made it! I guess the secret to a successful ARC is to have a good boat and a good skipper. In the event we had a great boat and a great skipper and a great crew and a great time. End of story.

22 DECEMBER FOLLOW UP

Colin has just texted our results. We were 4th in our class (Class C). *Nutcracker* won the Oyster prize. *Adeia* won the blog prize. The overall results aren't published yet but looking at the corrected times we're about 28th. Colin has apparently gone to celebrate with his traditional virulent curry.

After much squabbling to choose the winners of the competitions we called in Andrew Bishop of the ARC and Elaine Bunting of Yachting World for an unbiased opinion. They chose as follows:

The Naming Colin's Cafe Competition was won by John Kingsley with his excellent 'Heads, You Win'.

The answer to the question 'Why did the chicken cross the Atlantic?' was amazingly won by myself with 'To try out his fowl weather gear'.

So what have our brave crew been doing since the last blog?

Poled-out Jenny is continuing her search for the ideal man. *The Telegraph* rejected her advert in the Kindred Spirits section 'Powerful well-cut female, draft forward, seeks partner to extend her. Twin poles an advantage'. So she is reduced to cruising the world's jetties looking for someone who eats carbon fibre for breakfast and stows on the right.

Samantha sadly decided that Lotsa Luca was only after one thing – her mind. This not being her strong suit, she has decided to look for more uplifting work and has returned to St Lucia hoping to become a trainee blog writer. An accountant has resolved her initial confusion over the term 'syntax'.

Birgit has been with the Bond team for some weeks now but has only just met Daniel. Sadly, her opening gambit 'Oh James, let's go for re-entry on ARC 2007' fell wide of the mark and she has been relegated to the copywriting department. Her classic '007, licensed to kill and sell cigarettes' has already passed into Hollywood folklore.

The rest of the Cru are winding down towards Christmas. Colin has nearly finished a set of watercolours of the various ARC weather regions (Kate, Olga etc.) entitled Rain and Marmite Later, Good. John has repatriated his collection of suppositories, although we didn't enquire how he got them through customs (Alimentary, my dear Watson). David continues his quest to make the sextant sexy (Just pull the sun down to the horizon, Samantha). After 3000 miles of tweaking, Paul is just the man to sort out a turkey with all the trimmings. Tim, pictured in the team photo hiding under the sprayhood, has finally found his shorts.

Finally, we would like to wish all our readers a very happy Christmas and thank you for your support. It will come in very handy when the shrouds finally chafe through.

SKIPPER VS CREW,

CREW VS SKIPPER

Clashes, quarrels and contests
between skipper and crew!

TIM DAVISON
Illustrations by John Quirk

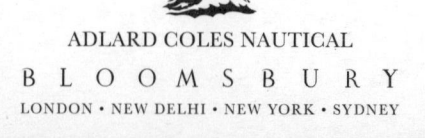

ADLARD COLES NAUTICAL

B L O O M S B U R Y

LONDON • NEW DELHI • NEW YORK • SYDNEY

Published by Adlard Coles Nautical
an imprint of Bloomsbury Publishing Plc
50 Bedford Square
London
WC1B 3DP
www.adlardcoles.com

ISBN: 978-1-4081-5413-7
ePub ISBN: 978-1-4081-5904-0
ePDF ISBN: 978-1-4081-5592-9

A CIP catalogue record for this book is available from the British Library.

This book is produced using paper that is made from wood grown in managed,
sustainable forests. It is natural, renewable and recyclable. The logging and
manufacturing processes conform to the environmental regulations of the
country of origin.

Typeset in Legacy Serif ITC 9.75pt on 12.25pt
Printed and bound in the UK by Clays Ltd.

Note: while all reasonable care has been taken in the publication of this book, the
publisher takes no responsibility for the use of the methods or products described
in the book

DISCLAIMER

While the information contained in this book is believed to be correct at the
time of publication, the publishers and author make no representation, express
or implied, with regard to the accuracy, adequacy or completeness of the
information contained herein. Every reasonable effort has been made to trace
copyright holders of material reproduced in this book but if any have been
inadvertently overlooked the publishers would be grateful to hear from them.

❄ CONTENTS ❄

SKIPPER vs CREW

To Judith, who had the original idea, then had to put up
with my experimental quips ... for a year!
And to Simon and Chloe, my dream crew.

INTRODUCTION

WHAT THEY SAID ABOUT *SKIPPER vs CREW*!

'Absolute rubbish' *Community Infill Monthly*
'The author does not quite pull it off' *Lingerie Review*
'Vry funy. Yew wil larf alowd' *Dyslexia Digest*
'Unsuitable for the older reader' *Gravedigger Weekly*
'Unsuitable for the younger reader' *Acne News*
'Unsuitable' *Bespoke Tailor*
'Not an approach to yachting of which we approve' *Blue Ensign*
'Provocative' *Ramrod International*
'Very slow to take off' *Royal Poona Airline Inflight Magazine*

In these pages you will be given good, sound, nautical advice. No doubt, like most sailors, you will ignore it. You will press ahead and buy a ruinously expensive boat, crew her with a bunch of misfits and set off for wildly optimistic destinations. Only when you have sorted out the inevitable shambles will you return to the wisdom contained herein.

THE AUTHOR

Tim Davison set out to be a nautical author but slipped off the bottom of the learning curve. His boats have ranged from a converted dustbin lid (it sank) to a radio-controlled model yacht (it got stuck in the bushes). In between he has owned 19 Lasers (in the hope that the next one would go faster), several Laser IIs and a 470 – in which he managed to come last in the Olympic Trials.

Denied racing success he decided to apply his 'round the buoys and back to the girls' philosophy to the world of cruising. This caused innumerable disasters, since cruising should be a subtle and thoughtful occupation. Luckily his boat has a lifting keel or he would still be aground somewhere in Brittany. He hopes this book will help you avoid some of his hairier cock-ups, but is resigned to your finding new and interesting ways to embarrass yourselves.

THE SKIPPER'S RULES

Skippering is a bit like managing a company. First, tell the team what The Rules are. Then enforce them ruthlessly. That should stamp out initiative and creativity, leaving you unchallenged at the top of the heap.

Display The Rules. Then keep emphasizing the points – and watch morale improve!

RULE 1
Don't bring me a problem unless you've tried to fix it.

RULE 2
If you can't fix it, at least hold the torch while I have a try.

RULE 3
If I can't fix it, it's obviously a very complex problem calling for a skilled professional at the height of his powers.

RULE 4
Hints don't work. If you want to go ashore, reduce sail, or tack so you're in the sun, just ask. In any case, the answer's no.

RULE 5
I like to wear my mid-layer to dinner, and shorts when sightseeing. Just humour me.

RULE 6
If I'm concentrating, it's because I'm racing someone. If they're faster, our bottom must be dirty. If they're slower, it's because I did the Olympic Trials in 1972.

RULE 7
Don't ask what's in my mind unless you want to hear about forestay tension, coppercoat vs antifouling or my nifty manoeuvre in Cowes Week. Then at least pretend to be interested.

RULE 8
Bring essentials with you. We won't be putting ashore to buy lipstick, hair gel or slinky shorts. What do you think this is, a holiday?

RULE 9

It costs an extra £50,000 for a boat 3ft longer. No, I'm not thinking of upgrading so you can bring an extra kitbag.

RULE 10

Learn to use the toilet. It's not that hard. And if you block it, the snorkels are in the stern locker.

RULE 11

Don't wear your lifejacket under your oilskins. If it inflates you will suffocate and the Racing Rules state we have to start and finish with the same number of (live) crew.

RULE 12

If I've just spent a couple of hours changing the engine oil or unblocking the toilet, it's probably not my turn to do the washing up.

RULE 13

The boat comes first, so don't expect mollycoddling. (This rule can only be broken if the skipper is cold, wet or hungry, when it's obviously vital to make sure the man at the top is comfortable.)

'It might be better to wear your lifejacket outside your oilies ...'

RULE 14

Any complaints about the boat, the navigation, the bunks or the food should in the first instance be made to the bosun. If the bosun is married to the skipper, forget it – the complaints will already have been made.

(After sticking this list onto the chart table it may be wise to take a walk ashore while the crew discuss their joy at finding you such a thoughtful and sensitive leader.)

'I think it's your turn to wash up, Skipper ...'

I'M SORRY I HAVEN'T A CLEW

I'm Sorry I Haven't a Clue® is my favourite panel game, particularly the section where the team give alternative definitions to words. But would this work with nautical terms?

See what you think: the words are taken from the publisher's guidelines to budding authors. (It may help to read the words out loud.)

WORD	ALTERNATIVE DEFINITION
Abaft the beam	Buttocks
Athwart	A lisping pimple
Backwater	A shower
Bow wave	Acknowledging applause
Callsign	Beckoning motion from a call girl
Cap shroud	How to keep your hat on
Centreplate	Denture for front teeth
Chain plate	Impractical crockery design
Channel 16	A disappointing perfume
Chart datum	A liaison with the navigator
Clockwise	Someone who can tell the time
Clove hitch	Lack of spices in the galley
Companionway	How to get your squeeze below
Cross-current	An out-of-sorts sultana
Crosstrees	A felled forest
Danbuoy	A sailor in a Robin Reliant
De-rig	Cool Caribbean clothes
Dead reckoning	A pension adviser
Deadrise	Easter
Deckhead	A posh idiot
Delamination	To become excited about an agreement
Depth sounder	To break wind while swimming
Dipstick	To capsize
Doldrums	Ancient timpani
Dover Strait	A flat Dover Sole
Draught	To get the wind up in shallow water
Drop keel	A bad mistake
Eyesplice	The wedding of two oculists
Flat-bottomed	Girls that make the world go round
Flying bridge	A game played in aeroplanes
Focsle	Your parents' backsides
Fore-and-aft	4.5
Forecabin	Where foreplay takes place
Forestay	Being ill in your cabin

Foul weather	Too stormy for chickens
Fresh water	H_2 Oh!
Fully-battened	A corset
Gelcoat	What a Jelly Baby wears
Ground tackle	To sit down
Gunwale	A vengeful fish
Half decker	A weak punch
Handbearing compass	A donkey with a gruesome present
Hand over hand	A faulty bacon slicer
Hard-wearing	Dragging the dinghy up the ramp
Hawse pipe	Portsmouth Poll's briar
Head wind	A sneeze
Heads	Gambling in the lavatory
Heave-to	Both your crew are sick
In stays	The corsetier's profession
Kilowatt	A big question
Knock-down	A boat jumble
Latitude	An opinionated Frenchman
Leech	A small animal clinging to the sail
License	Trying to knock some sense into a louse
Lifebuoy	An imprisoned channel marker
Lifejacket	Dad's Harris Tweed
Lifting strop	An angry Bosun's Chair
Lighthouse	An arsonist
Lighting board	A bored arsonist
Lock-keeper	A frugal hairdresser
Loose-footed	Fred Astaire
Lugsail	A hearing aid auction
Mole wrench	Tweezers
Morse code	Oxford manners
Ocean cruiser	A mermaid
Oilskin	Olive Oyl's family
Outdrive	Where to leave a stately home
Over-sheeted	Corpse
Over canvassed	Bored members of a focus group
Overfall	A drunken skipper
Pan Pan	Instructions to a photographer
Pier head	An idiot of your own age
Porthole	The crew's mouth after dinner
Pre-stretch	In custody
PRUDONCE	A stupid insurance salesman
Pulpit	What to do with this book
Sand bar	A pub on the beach

Sandbank	Where you get the cash to go to the sand bar
Sea shore	Hard cockpit cushions
Seawards	Places for ill sailors
Seaweed	A feeble crew
Self-steering	A sober sailor
Semiconductor	A musician with a spike on his head but wearing Wellingtons
Sheer legs	Crew in tights
Sheet	A term of surprise
Shock-cord	A flat note
Short-handed	A Scotsman's pockets
Short-wave	A disinterested goodbye
Slipway	How to do the moonwalk
Sparbuoy	A supermarket stacker
Split pin	A tiny axe
Sports inflatables	A lifesaving bra
Steep-to	Expensive
Stemhead	The idiot at the bow
Strum box	A guitar
Tidetable	Preventing the furniture moving about
Toe rail	To swear when you hurt your foot
Topmark	Scratching the hull
Under power	A negligee
Under canvas	A scratchy vest
Undertow	A shoe
Unship	Harmony between Uns
Uptide	Lashed to the mast
Up to date	London singles club
Waterfront	A beer belly
Waterline	A nautical come-on
Weather helm ...	... are my spectacles?
Well-found	A rich dog
Wetsuit	A wimpish executive
Windex	A former sailing partner
Windvane	Makeup for sailors
Yardarm	Size XL

Sports inflatables

Now here are some to try for yourself:

Backwinding	Lookout	Quick flashing	Stern gland
Give way	Pickup buoy	Sailbag	Trade winds
Laying up	Propshaft	Sleeping bag	Upwash

If they don't like your puns, try sailing singlehanded. A case of *I'm Sorry I Haven't a Crew*, perhaps.

BUNKMATES

The dating column for members of the Lower Trousers Yacht Club.

SKIPPERS SEEKING CREW

Back eddy. Unsuccessful racing skipper, only one conviction for manslaughter, seeks crew who are no strangers to the terms 'unfair handicap', 'waypoint error' and 'uncontrollable crying'. Knowledge of team building and resuscitation an advantage. Box 999

Skipper and part-time taxidermist looking for experienced crew to sail 13m ketch to Tahiti. Failing that, anyone still warm and vertical may apply. You will almost certainly get the job. And will probably return in your own skin. Box 7752

Scrimshaw exam invigilator whose passions include red shorts, constructing chocolate shackles and discussing rig tension seeks first mate to help pass long nights at anchor. If you have your own black ball and LED torch we are made for each other. No time wasters. Box 5620

My hobbies include incomprehension and engine maintenance. Often, I indulge both together. If you are the sort of crew who finds rust a challenge and welcomes a socket set for Christmas, marry me and we will make the diesel beat faster. Box 8871

Dinosaur needs nerdy crew to stop the depth warning beeping. Also, how can we prevent the Navtex listing Norwegian cable-laying manoeuvres? A working knowledge of programming chartplotters is required, or at least experience of how to enter a Route without going over the green bits. In return I offer dark hair, hazel eyes and a zest for zumba dancing. Box 5567

Not all that blisters is osmosis. Amateur philosopher, lone sailor, deprived of human contact since the heads shower broke, now rather lonely. If you share my interest in sewage treatment, toad breeding and Nietzsche and know how to keep a severed finger operable, our long night watches will flash by. M, 46, Box 4490

Too many evenings spent manoeuvering the little plastic boats from the rules book? Now you're ready for some action. A qualified barrister, QC or judge sought to join our team and take control of protests, spring drunken crew from custody and help the skipper avoid speeding fines. Ability to sail an advantage, but not essential. Interviews, in your wig please, at Little Higginbottom S.C. on Saturday. Box 6643

Help me teak oil my collection of wooden bungs. Fastidious skipper, Slocum lookalike but never yet ventured outside Broadstairs Harbour, seeks crew for inaugural voyage to Ramsgate. Must be prepared to re-use teabags. Box 4448

Virgo would like to meet Libra (Male to 50). Would also consider Piscean with Plastimo dinghy or a Taurean with own paint roller and boiler suit. Or even a Capricorn with a sister called Elsie. Frankly it's been a quiet year so far, but with Uranus rising that is all about to change. Check your horoscope then contact me at Box 6112.

If complete deadlock is your experience with skipper/crew relations you won't be disappointed on our boat, *Schadenfreude*. We train in an atmosphere of mistrust and recrimination, seeing this as the perfect preparation for our Annual Cruise. Endorsements from former crew range from 'Intolerable' via 'Incompetent' to 'Lucky to Survive'. Surprisingly, a crew vacancy has arisen. Send your CV to Box 9901.

CREW SEEKING SKIPPERS

Think of a cohesive team of fit, tanned, good-humoured and experienced sailors for whom the description 'willing and responsible crew' might have been invented. We're nothing like that, but if you're really desperate and your boat doesn't leak, contact Box 3321.

My eyes are a delicate blue but so is the rest of me. Skipper with Eberspacher sought by hypothermic crew. I come with my own mid-layer and hip flask. Box 9664

Slim, blonde Scandinavian beauty seeks skipper for nights of tinkering with the engine, making the anchor light work and trying to switch to the other gas cylinder. Seriously though, contact Pete at Box 3347 if you've finally decided to get real.

Very tall man available to crew on boat with good headroom. I am experienced in spreader repair, re-threading halyards and judging the height of bridges. I have many uses in shallow water and have often been asked to push off. Can double as spare spinnaker pole and replacement mizzen mast. Contact Lofty at Box 7790.

Join the crew's union. Is your skipper impossible? Is he a contender for the Foulmouth Award? Do you need emotional support? Fight back with The Crew's Union. Our insurance covers psychotherapy, lost winch handles and dropped fenders, and GBH cover is available for when you need to get physical. Plus we guarantee to find you another ride if your union membership gets you dropped. Box 208, Keynsham, Bristol

Casanova was a librarian. Honest, caring librarian, dewey-decimal compliant, neaped in the returns department seeks sincere skipper for re-launch and maybe more. Looks not important but must like goldfish on board. Overdue fines quashed for genuine friend/soulmate. Bucks. Box 6609

My friends can't understand what I see in you. But from the moment I stepped onto the acres of teak deck under your 52m mast I knew, somehow I just knew. Please contact me. I promise not to be sick again on the upholstery. Box 2275

Baggywrinkles? Country bumpkin? Old gaffer? Neaped or tucked? Nobody's perfect and you can still find a skipper to love with our confidential service. We are especially effective in the fitting out season. And do try our tailored boiler suits. Contact Dogs Afloat at Box 5331.

When you reply to this ad your sailing life will never be the same again. You will hear words like Course to Steer, error, rocks and A&E – in the same sentence. And you know you've always wanted to launch a liferaft. Accident-prone crew seeks berth for the summer. Comes with own lifejacket, Williamson stretcher and parachute flares. Might also be worth mentioning that I was Miss Portugal last year. Box 4509

BOATS SEEKING BOATS
Eat my wake. Tender wanted by old gaffer (36ft overall) with cute transom. Genuine articles only – no inflatables. Hamble. Box 1357

BOATS SEEKING TLC
The Incredible Hulk. *Spray* look-alike, slim hull and pre-bent rig, enjoys overseas travel and quiet evenings at anchor WLTM handy owner for long term relationship. If you are very rich, have a diploma in woodwork and a GSOH (gigantic shed with own heater) write to Box 9871. Lying constantly.

Tender Behind. Six foot pram with hard thwarts seeks a new home. Comes with own rowlocks. You have absolutely nothing to lose except your no-claim bonus. Box 5643

SURVEY: ARE YOU A SKIPPER OR A CREW?

Napoleon maintained that every Private carries a Field Marshall's baton in his backpack. In the same way every crew probably carries a skipper's logbook in his oilies.

On the other hand, judging by the turnips on the tiller you will encounter, there are many skippers who should carry a crew's manual in their blazer pockets.

So, to which of life's bunks are you best suited – the stately stern cabin or the precarious pipecot?

This survey will help predict your station in life. If you are an Elephant and Castle, worry not; being a humble crew will save you loads of misery and money. But if you are a Knightsbridge you obviously have the necessary wedge and enjoy delegating all the chores. It doesn't matter, the key thing is to be in the right slot.

Here we go. For each of the questions below, choose one answer: **A**, **B** or **C**. Then use the key at the end to calculate your score and your destiny. Good luck!

1. Your replacement on watch is so sound asleep you can't wake him. Do you:
   A Make a ringing noise, then say 'It's Michelle Pfeiffer for you ...'
   B Put on a scary mask and climb into his bunk.
   C Remove a fistful of fivers from his wallet as a forfeit.

2. You can't get the chartplotter to store your carefully entered route. Do you:
   A Thump it.
   B Say 'We'll use traditional methods today – you never know when the GPS may fail.'
   C Call your nine-year-old for advice.

3. You drop your mobile in the water. Do you:
   A Tape it to the top of the engine to dry out.
   B Switch to Skype on your Kindle.
   C Insist someone else lends you their phone.

4. You collide with a three-ton safe water mark in the dark. Do you:

A Phone your mother.

B Start bailing.

C Report a buoy out of position.

5. You misinterpret the weather forecast and get hit by a Force 8. Do you:

A Make yourself some waterproofs by punching arm and leg holes in a couple of sailbags.

B Use the saloon curtains as a neck towel.

C Bluster that it's a good opportunity to test for leaks.

The skipper's religious beliefs often surfaced in Force 8

6. Coming back from lunch ashore you find the dinghy has a serious puncture. Do you:

A Blow it up and swim around looking for bubbles.

B Buy a lilo from the tobacconists and paddle that back to the boat.

C Leave it to be stolen, hitch a ride back aboard and phone your insurance company.

7. The hatch in your cabin leaks. Do you:

A Sleep in your waterproofs.

B Bung it up with chewing gum.

C Order the youngest person aboard to swap cabins.

8. There are two inches of smelly water in the bottom of the fridge. Do you:

A Use the sump-oil extractor to suck it out.

B Tip in some rice to absorb it and make a risotto.

C Save the liquid for soup.

9. A seacock rusts through and falls out. Water is gushing in. Do you:

A Ignore it and put your passport and wallet into a waterproof bag.

B Push a carrot into the hole.

C Hammer in a softwood bung and pour everyone a stiff gin.

10. When you drain the engine the liquid is a mixture of oil and water. Do you:
   A Say it's pretty and reminds you of marbling.
   B Take a Valium.
   C Put the boat on the market.

11. You miscalculate the tide and arrive at the bar to find only 20cm of water. Do you:
   A Go below and read a book.
   B Hitch a ride ashore on a passing sailing dinghy.
   C Phone the almanac people and complain the tide tables are wrong.

12. As you arrive for the weekend cruise the phone rings and one person cancels. Do you:
   A Cross the road to the pub and ask for volunteers.
   B Buy a round in the pub and ask for volunteers.
   C Buy drinks for the whole evening and take your pick of the volunteers.

13. You run aground and the boat lies on her side. Do you:
   A Go below and watch a DVD.
   B Pad one side of your bunk so you can snooze on the level.
   C Step overboard with a broom and pretend you planned to dry out so you can scrub the bottom.

KEY
Each time you chose **A** score 1 point, **B** = 2 points or **C** = 3 points.

Your profile
Score 13–19. You are self-centred, lazy and dim. Excellent skipper material.
Score 20–29. You have clearly done a bit of sailing but haven't quite learned how to avoid work. Best to crew on a variety of boats and learn how it's done.
Score 30+. Congratulations! Your deviousness makes Machiavelli look like an amateur. You can choose to be either a divisive crew or a manipulative skipper and should manage to ruin the harmony on any sailing boat.

THE SKIPPERS' CLUB

The Skippers' Club was founded in response to The Crew's Union (see *Crew vs Skipper*, page 20).

MISSION STATEMENT
Non illigitimum carborundum (don't let the bast**ds grind you down).

OBJECTIVES
The main objective of the Club is to become a centre of excellence for the traditional values of a skipper at sea, i.e. seasickness, superiority and shabbiness.

To assist members in perfecting these skills the clubhouse will have low ceilings, small damp beds, warm beer and a swear box.

FLAG ETIQUETTE
The club pennant shall be worn at the masthead. It consists of a green background with carrot-coloured dots (representing seasickness), incorporating code flag 'V' (signifying superiority) and a ragged fly (for shabbiness).

The ensign is similar but the hoist is defaced by its own petard.

ELIGIBILITY
A prospective member must meet at least two of the following criteria:
Has sailed a minimum of 1000 hours at sea, with more than half spent asleep
Has made a passage of at least 30 miles, but arrived in the wrong port
Has been sued for incompetence by a crew member
Has been boarded by police after a complaint about foul language
Has a close relation in the wine trade
Was once mistaken for Joshua Slocum, Bluebeard or Popeye

Members' benefits include training courses such as:
- Master before God: A practical look at weddings, burials and keelhauling
- Psychology in the cockpit: Humble the crew the Kierkegaard way
- Using the blunderbuss for pleasure and profit
- Karate: A holistic approach
- 100 days in a dinghy: A positive approach to mutiny
- Ropecraft for the busy skipper. We show how to make baggywrinkle, a spare pair of braces and a hangman's noose

Ropecraft for the busy skipper

- Health and Safety Afloat. An intensive course on men overboard, women overboard and fenders overboard. Deciding which to recover first. The kiss of life. How to re-inflate a fender. A section on suppositories may be inserted
- Engine maintenance. Your diesel is your best friend, and with a little attention it will always look after you. We explain why you should get out more
- A historic approach to navigation. Astrolabes are provided
- Emergencies at sea. Our instructor has experience of swamping, grounding, dismasting, sinking, colliding and fire on board. He now teaches shore-based courses only

Other benefits include discounts on the Club's publications:

Ruthless: A guide to effective skippering

Changing Anodes: An underwater guide

Sea Shanties (complete with plastic accordion and earplugs)

Blocked: Nautical loos through the ages

The Leadership Secrets of Knud the Impaler (comes with free wooden bung)

A Skipper's Guide to Obfuscation: When they're in the dark they can't argue

PRETTY PROFILES

THE WEALTHY SKIPPER

Everything on Jonathan's yachts is electric and can be remotely controlled by a joystick on his office desk. It's startling for the crew when, on passage, *Government Subsidy* suddenly alters course, the gennaker unrolls and she sets off for a nearby port to pick up a business contact.

Time is money in the city. To avoid wasting it he orders the crew to set sail, then boards his helicopter on the office roof and directs the pilot to drop him into the sea near the boat. The crew pick him up, he sails for an hour, jumps in again, the chopper recovers him and he's flown back to his desk. Thus he fills the gap between London closing and Tokyo coming on stream.

Apart from these jaunts, he only uses the boat one month a year. The rest of the time he beavers away at his desk ten hours a day, while the crew luxuriate on 'their' yacht in the sunshine. The irony of this escapes him.

He met Samantha when she was working at a Gucci party at the America's Cup. She was in full evening dress with killer heels and was dripping diamonds. The only way to get rid of her security minder was to buy the lot. Once on the balcony, Jonathan lost no time in proposing and during the ensuing negotiation promised to buy her a yacht. *Government Subsidy* was delivered just in time for the honeymoon.

The broker told him he shouldn't spend more than 10% of his wealth on a yacht, so the £30 million price tag was well within budget. Sadly, this changed during the refit – Samantha insisted the mahogany panelling be replaced with something darker, the crew demanded Titanium winches and the en-suites needed gold taps. Just the bill for flowers in the cabins would support an African state for a month. The boat now looks like a floating Harrods and he's working 12 hours a day.

Jonathan has finally got a yacht so big he can't get onto it. Part of the crew's brief is to position the steps when he returns from a party at the Costa Smeralda Yacht Club loaded with shopping and business cards. But from the towering deck saloon he can keep an eye on rivals' yachts and monitor the comings and goings of their guests. More than once this has paid off when he's spotted a clandestine takeover meeting and immediately bought shares via his yacht's satellite communications centre. This also comes in handy for watching Hogtown United's games (he bought the club from a Russian oligarch with last year's bonus).

Very occasionally he thinks back to his time as a lad in a Topper. He could bike to the sailing club, drift up the river and eat his Mars Bar when he chose. Money never came into it. Yachts never came into it. Samantha never came into it. Life seemed all so simple then.

LE SKIPPEUR FRANÇAISE

SKIPPEUR Bonjour matelote. Bienvenue aboard.
Vous avez l'experience de sailing?

CRU Oui. Mon oncle a un Laser.

SKIPPEUR Bien. S'il vous plait allez below
et calculez la course pour
Cherbourg.

CRU Cherbourg? C'est un dump.

SKIPPEUR Dur luck, j'ai un rendez-vous
avec un oiseau là.

(La cru calcule et revient au deck)

CRU Conduissez 185

SKIPPEUR 185 vrai?

CRU Certainment vrai. Je ne
vous donne une course
faux!

SKIPPEUR Non, non. 185 vrai ou magnetique?

CRU 185 vrai. Environs 190 magnetique.

SKIPPEUR Vous souvenez le deviation?

CRU Deviation, variation. C'est comme le porno ici.

SKIPPEUR Vous êtes un twit. Grippez le tiller, je vais checker pour moi-
même.

CRU OK. Je pousse pour tourner left, tirer pour tournez droit?

SKIPPEUR Blow ceci pour un jeu de soldiers. Mais oui, c'est ca.

CRU Bon. C'est une piece de gateau, le sailing.

(Le skippeur checks la course et revient dans le pit de poulet.)

SKIPPEUR Bien. J'ai mis un waypoint sur le chartplotter.

CRU Je conduisez le petit bateau vers le X?

SKIPPEUR Oui.

CRU Et les purple bits?

SKIPPEUR C'est le radar overlay. Les bateaux purple sont les tanqueurs.
Avoidez-les a tout cost.

CRU Je suis avec vous la, mate. Get votre tete en bas pour un couple
d'heures si vous aimez.

SKIPPEUR Merci. Prenez un bon lookout.

(Apres une heure il y a un crash terrible)

CRU Je m'excuse. J'ai pris un catnap pour un moment et ce tanqueur a
frappe notre cote starboard!

SKIPPEUR	Vous vraiment prenez le biscuit! Launchissez le raft de vie.
CRU	Ok. Peut etre grabbez l'EPIRB et des ingots de chocolat?
SKIPPEUR	Oui. Un stitch en temps save neuf, eh?

(*Dans le raft de vie*)

SKIPPEUR	C'est un peu comme un waterbed!
CRU	Ne devenez frisky. C'est un situation serieux.
SKIPPEUR	Ok. Ok. Anyway, vous n'êtes pas ma type.

(*Il prend son telephone mobile.*) 'Sophie? C'est moi. Domage, je sera un peu tard pour dinner. Et peux-tu alerter les services de rescue? Tres bien. Nous attendons. C'est les last orders? Ok, je prend un pepper steak. Au point, avec frites et salade. Et une bouteille de vin rouge. St Emillion – le 2003 si possible. Tres bien, merci.

CRU	Tres chic Claude. Les premiers choses premier, eh?

THE FRAFFLY SMART SKIPPER

SKIPPER	Au kay, paya tension
CREW	Oh no, what now?
SKIPPER	The playn is to sell via Caes to Alderneh Wind twenteh neots NE. Eea teea ayah sivin tomorr oh. Any kestions?
CREW	Do we have to go?
SKIPPER	Yeass, wren or shane
CREW	Do we have enough diesel?
SKIPPER	Gellons
CREW	And enough food?
SKIPPER	Eneaph to feid an armeh
CREW	What about watches?
SKIPPER	Tu orn, tu orf
CREW	Shall we book a berth in the marina?
SKIPPER	Emma chisit?
CREW	£30 a night
SKIPPER	Au kay, tu niets then. Staynd bay to cassd orf ...

THE SAGA SKIPPER

Ever since she moved to St Peter's Close (!), Vera has given up going on deck. She contents herself with navigating from the chart table and writing cheques to cover the racing breakages. Although she owns the boat, she leaves the tactics and tuning to the nice man from Hellava Draft Sails who sold her a complete set of Mylar headsails, thus revolutionising *Zimmer*'s performance. On a good day, using Vera's 70-year experience of the Solent, they can take a podium position.

Otherwise, her greatest joy is reminiscing about sailing in the Good Old Days. Once, aground on the Brambles Bank for an entire tidal cycle, she invited each member of the foredeck in turn to come below for a drop of Dunkirk Spirit and to hear about her experiences in boats confiscated from the Third Reich. The rest of the crew escaped to the cockpit where they concocted a complicated scoring system based on length of time below, quantity of alcohol consumed and loudness of snoring. The eventual winner was 'Creepy' Jones (so named because he lives in Crawley), who emerged after a marathon chinwag clutching an empty Scotch bottle and singing something unintelligible about Rommel's anatomy.

This incident has revolutionised *Zimmer*'s offshore performance. Unwilling to risk going below, the crew sleep on the windward rail all night, powering the boat to the finish. The only downside is that they are usually asleep for the prize-giving, leaving Vera to consume the entire boat's ration of free grog.

As a token effort at team building, the Skipper holds a crew dinner once a year. She makes her entrance on a battered Harley Davidson, peeling off her leathers to reveal a sequinned cocktail dress and long black gloves. Holding a Balkan Sobranie in an elegant cigarette holder, she directs 'her boys' in a series of drinking games not seen since the Battle of Britain.

Blindfolded and trying to pin a moustache on Hitler's photo, the crew wonder if there isn't another boat they could sail on next season. Sadly, skills learned at Vera's knee (and other low joints) don't readily transfer to a modern ocean racer, a condition known in the trade as Being Zimmer Framed.

THE NAME'S POND, JAMES POND

Hi Colin

I got your email about lack of racing in the winter. I agree, a long layoff is a pain but there is one way to keep your hand in, keep warm and to guarantee success in the new season.

No, I am not referring to dating debutants but to the ancient sport of model yacht racing. Forget about sunhats and the Round Pond in Kensington. They have radio-controlled boats now. You get maybe ten races in a morning and that means 10 starts, 10 gybe marks and 10 opportunities to curse the opposition. Half a season's entertainment in half a day.

The first thing you'll need is...new glasses! It's tricky to spot your boat in the crowd at the windward mark 100 metres away. You'll find yourself sailing down the reach beautifully, but halfway along the boat stops responding and it gradually dawns that you have been trying to sail someone else's. The next problem is locating your own boat! Often it's in the trees the other side of the pond, or stuck in the reeds where you can't get at it. For some reason the other skippers find this very funny. New specs help a lot.

Frequency is the next thing. Not the kind that old Crafty used to suffer from at school but the number on the little chip in your radio. Make sure that no-one else is on your wavelength or you will suddenly find your boat tacking when you're steering straight. Or ploughing straight into the pond's concrete wall when your rudder control is hard over. Again, good entertainment for the troops.

You will find that walking along the bank keeps you closer to the boat and makes things easier to judge. However, if you're looking at the boat beware plunging in when the bank takes a turn. And if you do, surface with a timely comment such as: 'Got it! Knew I'd lost the rudder about here last week.' While walking always hold your transmitter horizontally so the aerial sticks out forwards. That way you have the pleasure of stabbing anyone in front of you who slows down for an instant. Plus there is the opportunity of some nifty swordplay with skippers doing the same thing coming the other way. And a final trick is to walk so your personal windshadow projects onto your opponent's sail. Many an overlap has been gained like this.

You can always spot a model yotter by his claw-like hands, which have spent the regatta locked around the transmitter. Further clues are a tennis visor, thick glasses, waders, a bag of spares and a little stick with a hook for lifting the boat out. Despite the elegance of this rigout, there aren't many females in the fleet. The upside of this is that you will be able to concentrate fully on speed, tactics and abusive language. Let me know how you get on.

Yours aye

Tim

I SEA WHAT YOU MEAN

If communication is difficult on land, it's almost impossible at sea. Just remember the cardinal skipper's rule: shout louder and louder until someone understands.

Even when hopelessly out of his depth, the good skipper puts on a brave face – then lies through his teeth.

In case you want to know what he really means, here's a quick crib.

WHAT THE SKIPPER SAYS	WHAT THE SKIPPER MEANS
Bit draughty!	I'm not sure I can handle this
Would you like to go back?	I'd like to go back
Let's clip on!	If anyone falls off in this, they're dead
The GPS is on the blink again	I'm lost
Take a look through the binocs.	Can you see ANYTHING?
That must be the buoy	Please let it be the buoy
It's a North Cardinal	So why's there no topmark?
You look like a real sailor	Those oilskins are enormous!
You seem to have thought of every eventuality	Where are we going to stow all that?
Nice to have a choice of swimsuits	Why would anyone need SIX?
Wow! Amazing how ladies manage to look elegant after a long sail	I suppose I'd better change my jeans
Super hair and makeup, darling	We can't go to the greasy spoon then
She carries 250 litres of water	Time you guys had a shower
Can you keep your cabin doors closed?	The snoring has reached epic proportions
Retrieve the lazy guy	Pull the red one in a bit
Could you play the traveller?	Can't you see I've got the tiller behind my neck?
Keep an eye on the starboard boats.	How on earth do we get through that lot?
Water!	He probably won't fall for that old trick
Rule 93.3a, old boy	He might be stupid enough to fall for it
Ready about!	Yippee! He fell for it

THE CREW INTERVIEW

I was once interviewed for membership of a yacht club where the main criterion seemed to be: 'Would you like to spend a wet weekend in the cabin with this person?' Putting aside the thought that Pamela Anderson would probably have got in, this seemed a fair approach to putting together a convivial group.

For the cruising man it's even more important to select the right crew – you'll need someone who can do more than tie a bowline and smell nice on passage. So here are some suggestions for that all-important Crew Interview.

VENUE

Try to simulate the cruising environment. The room should obviously be cold, damp and darkish. Feed the interviewee something disgusting to promote nausea – jellied eels followed by desiccated coconut should do the trick. A saucer of diesel oil under the table will further enhance the ambience. If you can make the encounter tiring and frightening so much the better – maybe begin with a simulated marathon on a treadmill, with a defibrillator strapped to his chest.

An alternative tactic is to do the interview in your own home. This gives lots of opportunity to see if the intended victim is willing to help. Will he/she bring a bottle, help peel the potatoes, scrape food off the floor and offer to wash up? If he simply sits there giving you culinary advice and texting about the poor quality of the wine, the alarm bells should start ringing.

VERSATILITY

Obviously it's wise to ply him with loads of cheap plonk and brandy – there's going to be lots of that on the boat. After a litre or two, move on to after-dinner games. Trying to get round the room without touching the floor will give an idea of nimbleness; pinning the tail on the donkey when blindfolded will show if he can snorkel down to unblock the loo outlet; charades will indicate his ability to communicate from the foredeck in a gale.

INTELLIGENCE

A tricky one this. You want someone bright enough to be able to tackle all the nasty jobs on board, but not smart enough to quit and buy their own boat. A simple multiple choice test should reveal all.

1. You have been left alone on board with the skipper's wife. It's hot and she is sunbathing topless. Do you:
    A Start servicing the windlass to get a better look.

B Offer to rub teak oil onto her back.

C Ask if she will pose while you whittle a new figurehead.

2. You're on watch, it's rough and your supper is about to go over the side. Do you:

   A Swallow a handful of VomiNo pills, which immediately shoot out like grapeshot.

   B Ask where the bucket is kept, because you want to wash the cabin sole.

   C Pull out the airplane sick bag you always carry, and fill it neatly.

3. During the practice Man Overboard drill no-one manages to recover the fender that was tossed over the side. Do you:

   A Sink it with a well-aimed pellet from your air pistol, and sail on.

   B Send a Pan Pan for a new set of fenders to be waiting at your destination.

   C Dive over the side, resuscitate the fender and organise its recovery with a lifesling.

4. The skipper asks you to clip onto the lazy jack (he means the jackstay). Do you:

   A Clip on to it anyway, to show he's an idiot.

   B Tell him it's against your principles to take safety precautions.

   C Clip on and produce your personal EPIRB while whistling, 'Oh hear us when we cry to thee, For those in peril on the sea'.

5. The wind is building and you decide to drop the sails and use a sea anchor, only to discover that it's in the boot of the owner's car. Do you:

   A Use your mobile to call a lawyer and tell him to sue the owner.

   B Dismantle the toilet and use the bowl as a drogue, muttering, 'It could do with a wash anyway'.

   C Sacrifice your favourite sweater, tying a knot in each arm and holding the neck open with the ship's colander.

6. You are on deck and need to answer a call of nature. Do you:

   A Climb onto the pushpit and go for maximum range.

   B Reach into the companionway for a suitable container, such as a saucepan.

   C Ask the helmsman to heave-to while you go below.

KEY:
Score 1 for A, 2 for B and 3 for C

RESULTS
Score 6–9: You will go far in sailing, but not on our boat.

Score 10–13: You have the right idea, but lack experience. Spend more time on the computer playing Disastrous Deckhand.

Score 14+: You are too sophisticated for our boat and should check out the superyacht circuit.

YACHTING MEEKLY

Don't you hate those upbeat magazines, written by head boys and welding apprentices, with their can-do articles and ads for impossibly beautiful yachts?

The implication is that adding an exclamation mark turns any nautical cock-up into a simple project:

- You too can survive a hurricane in a Mirror dinghy!
- 300 professional meteorologists must be wrong! We teach you to trust your gut!
- Want to become a navigation expert? Just give us 30 seconds a day!
- Try Cape Horn for a fun-in-the-sun charter!
- Ditch your GPS! Why pencil and paper give greater accuracy
- Fitting out is quick and easy! We highlight the 674 essentials
- Collect egg-boxes and build a 36ft cruiser/racer!

No, what we need is a magazine for people like us, cack-handers who'd prefer root canal treatment to changing a cylinder head gasket, and who get breathless with worry before a trip to the fuel jetty.

In *Yachting Meekly* the articles will reflect our innate sense of worthlessness. A perfect issue would contain no exclamation marks and a consistently warped attitude to boat ownership:

- 101 Damnations: An appropriate curse for every job
- Face it, you're a bodger
- Zen and the art of ignoring osmosis
- Sail trim: Use wrinkles to give your boat character
- Living with leaks

... and so on. Plus there should be a sister magazine for the females in the crew, possibly more used to fashion glossies. *Pure Elle* would have features like:

- The wet look. Just peel off your oilskins and step ashore
- Your perfect weekend: Force 9 and sailing cancelled
- We try the 'Five Metre Wave' diet

- Scratch and sniff. WD40 is the new fragrance from Sid, yard manager of the year
- Exotic destinations: Why anywhere ashore will do
- Makeover in the quarterberth: Re-upholster those tired cushions to bring a sparkle to your cold, restless two hours off-watch
- Romance: If he's a closet sailor, run ...
- From catwalk to cap-shroud. We test Bosun's Chairs for comfort and style
- Hot shower offer of the month

These magazines will attract loads of advertising. After all, where else can you make angle-grinders, bankruptcy services and boiler-suits aspirational?

With the finances covered, all that remains is to find staff: photographers, designers and editors. But there's the rub: anyone in tune with the rags' ethos (Pasties, Pessimism and Procrastination) is unlikely to get things off the ground. Conversely, anyone with fire in their belly will inevitably alienate the readership. This could be the first fly in the varnish.

However, if you think you could be up to the job, and have a spare million to cover the launch issues, contact me c/o my literary agents Open, Read and Binnit.

Honestly, it's a winner. Just remember, no exclamation marks!!!!!!!!

HOW TO BE THE PERFECT SKIPPER

A good skipper has quiet authority and communicates clearly. He thinks ahead, giving himself enough time to explain what he wants before each manoeuvre begins, and what the escape route will be if things go wrong. He ensures everyone has a job, and treats the crew with respect. He himself is an experienced and highly competent sailor. His crew will go to the ends of the earth with him.

It's just conceivable that you fall slightly short of this ideal. If so, you will find important advice below. Follow it, and your crew will go to the ends of the earth with you (unless you put in to harbour, when they will probably get off).

NEVER TELL THEM ANYTHING

Confucius he say: 'Knowledge is power. Plus, if they don't know what's going on, they can't argue!'

As skipper, remember to be vague about the destination – if they can't tell whether it's a short hop or an all-nighter they will have to kerb their drinking, conserve water and keep the boat tidy. They may even show gratitude when you dock after only four hard hours thrashing to windward in Force 7.

Never explain how the toilet works, or if you do, make it incomprehensible. 'Before you begin open seacocks A to D, throw lever B to "Tank" and the small lever to the left. Give

three short pulls, three long ones then continue to pump normally until the bowl is half full. Never twist the handle or the nut may fall off the bottom. Now put the lever to the right and pump out the bowl. Hey presto, you're ready to begin! When you've finished, I'm afraid it's a bit more complicated ...' Most crew will now avoid using the contraption altogether and sit cross-legged with glazed eyes and rumbling innards. You will find them much easier to control like this.

Don't tell them where things are kept, or have a stowage plan. That way you are indispensable, especially when essentials like chocolate or beer are needed. The last thing you want is anyone having a good time without your taking the credit.

GIVE MISLEADING INSTRUCTIONS

You can have a lot of fun bawling people out for their mistakes, so you might as well ensure they make lots of them.

The trick is to give obscure instructions. 'You'll find the foghorn to the right of the table,' is excellent because it could be the saloon or chart table, and which way are you facing when it's on the right? You can then have a little rant when someone takes ten minutes to find it.

Similarly, 'Go to the mast and we'll put in a reef' sounds innocuous but they won't think to ask which reef until they're in place and then you can pretend not to hear the question. With one reef at the mast and three at the end of the boom you can enjoy a bit of cathartic hysteria.

Rushing up to the foredeck with a cry of 'Help me' is super, because it's not clear what you are trying to do up there. You could be planning to get the spinnaker ready, launch the dinghy or drop the anchor, for all they know. Whichever, you will certainly be able to berate them for slowness.

SHOUT A LOT

Don't just raise your voice, shout! And remember, although you're pretending to communicate, in fact you're pointing out their stupidity and your own superiority. Plus getting your own back for all the times you were shouted at by your mother, teacher, scout master and boss. Now you're really abusing your authority!

MUTINY

Day three of a cruise is crunch time, because by now they will be beginning to see through you. Regain control with a Skipper's Dinner. Bill this as a time when grievances can be aired in a civilised manner and solutions worked out by mutual consent. Of course that's the last thing you really want, so now is the time to uncork the bottles of cheap brandy you have been saving as paint stripper and mix some lethal cocktails. (Drink only Coke yourself – with a pink parasol in the glass they will assume you are matching them drink for drink.) Ask for helpful suggestions on how their

'holiday' can be improved. Half the crew will want to do more sailing, half spend more time ashore. Some will want two-hour watches, others four hours, and so on. With the jugs of firewater emptying and the discussion heading for World War 3 you can calmly take control – after all you are the only person who can talk without dribbling – and dress up your requirements as 'the best compromise'. And with a bit of luck you'll collect compliments for your sympathetic, consensual style. Take notes, because they won't remember much in the morning.

VIVE LA DIFFERENCE!

If your first language is French, your opportunities to score increase markedly. While speaking perfect English socially, lapse into rapid French when giving orders or sorting out mistakes. Your crew will stand rooted to the deck, at best reaching for Larousse. Shouting 'Ecoute', for example, is a masterstroke, because it could mean 'sheet in', 'sheet out', or 'listen'. Similarly 'Ris' could mean 'reef' or 'laugh' (though, being French, you may not see the funny side of this at the time). And 'Cap Terre' is not the point of land ahead, or even Terry's jaunty headgear, but the GPS readout 'Course Over The Ground'. They'll never get that one.

CREW CHANGES

Crew changes give an ideal opportunity to wound. Let's say two people are joining the boat, flying in to St Lucia Airport to replace another two who are leaving on the return flight. The crew will expect to be somewhere on the island the day before, giving time to get packed and find a taxi to the airport.

The clever skipper will procrastinate a few days earlier, maybe staying in port to 'fix the boat for a day or two,' and be nowhere near St Lucia as the deadline approaches. The crew will have to scurry to find a ferry or local flight to get to the international airport, struggle to find an ATM for the extra currency needed, and generally chaos will reign. Now you can have a great time saying you're afraid sailing is like that, you have to go with the vagaries of the wind and tide, that you're not running a bus service, etc. And all with no trouble to yourself!

With this much fun to be had, it's amazing that there are so few skippers in the world and so many crew. And that some of your victims come back trip after trip for more of The Treatment ...

I'M THE SKIPPER, YOU'RE THE CREW … GET OVER IT

If you have recently bought your own boat, life should be pretty rosy. At last you're the one giving the orders and they're the ones doing all the work.

In fact in the Navy you're told that the captain should be able to run the ship lying in his bunk with a broken leg, and I guess that should also be true for the skipper of a yacht (unless of course it was the crew who broke your leg in the first place).

With the purse strings in your hands you can start to get credit – even when it isn't due. For example, get the yard to do all the chores. Next weekend greet the crew with: 'Hello! I slipped down on Thursday evening to do a few jobs – please notice the radio aerial's been replaced, the navlights are working, we've got all new pipework in the heads and the stitching on the genoa's immaculate'. Accept the stunned silence as a compliment.

It's also your prerogative to set the boat's ethos. Many go for the 'Work hard and Play hard' approach, though this can backfire. I once sailed in a regatta on a boat where it was compulsory to race all day and party all night. On the fifth day the crew were so knackered they sailed straight into a navigation buoy, which smashed in the bow (and that was the last time they got smashed that week).

You also get to choose the crew, so you won't have to put up with someone else's auntie/mistress/bank manager. Choose an eclectic blend of talents to maximise the social fun: a pole dancer, a vicar and a journalist, for example.

But the main thing about acquiring skipper status is the long list of things you will never, ever, have to do again.

You will never have to:

- join in merry games like blow football, I-Spy something beginning with 'S', or strip snap
- see the dinghy tied to the stern of the yacht and have to swim across, ruining your moleskin underpants/Squadron socks or Tolpuddle YC tie.
- show off by drinking eight pints/climbing the mast/reciting Eskimo Nell (and, for maximum effect, attempt the triple)
- get completely soaked (except, sadly, in the financial sense)
- hide your toupee, *Beano* Annuals, spare hearing aid or Elvis CDs
- mind if they find your toupee, *Beano* Annuals, etc.
- go on the foredeck
- go on the sidedeck
- in fact, you need never leave the cockpit at all and should remain dapper, debonair and desirable (Ok, that may be stretching it a bit, but you should at least stay dry)
- take home your eyelash tongs/wellies/tanning cream (for that summer glow). Put these essentials in your cupboards – minor items like the First Aid kit, foghorn and tools can always go under the sink
- eat at someone else's favourite restaurant – so no more raw fish, yak steaks or pig's trotters
- worry about victualling the boat. Simply transfer all the stuff that's been lurking at the bottom of your fridge at home. At sea the crew aren't in a position to argue about sell by dates (except maybe the skipper's).
- share the onboard computer. It uses a lot of battery power, so insist it is saved for weather forecasts (under cover of which you can indulge in internet banking, joke swapping, emailing anecdotes about the crew, etc.)

Relish your new-found power and make sure they realise that, though it may be tough at the top, on your boat it's going to be even tougher at the bottom.

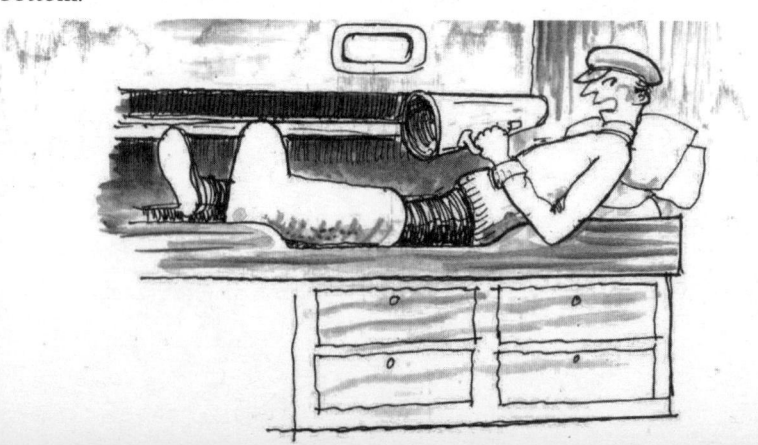

A RARE CHANCE TO OWN ...

A friend of mine is a yacht broker. Actually he sells superyachts, often with a price tag north of £30 million. One of his 'honest John' mottos is to advise his clients not to spend more than 10% of their wealth on a boat. They feel flattered, and he gets to know that they have another £270 million in reserve should the extras tot up the bill. 'Darling, for only another £400,000 we could have underfloor strobe lighting in the disco...'

For the rest of us, a budget of 10% of our net worth isn't going to make a boat builder's eyes light up. We'll be looking for a cheap second-hand craft, best found by spending lots of time in the pub reading the back pages of yachting magazines. Like estate agents' blurbs, these have a language all of their own, and it's important to know what the terms really mean.

TERM	MEANING
Extensive refit	Most of the rotten bits have been chopped out
Refurbished	A few rotten bits have been chopped out
A classic	None of the rotten bits have been chopped out
Well-equipped	Creature comforts consist of a cool bag and a portapotty
Comfortable	Excruciating without cushions
Recent survey	The last buyer pulled out
Well-maintained example	Needs loads of work each winter
Seaworthy	Needs a gale to get it going
A rare chance to own...	All the others have sunk
Blue water cruiser	Keel too deep to get into most marinas
Sailaway package	The engine has packed up
The yachtsman's choice	Your wife will hate it
For true sea lovers	Leaks
One owner	He couldn't sell it
Passionate	Desperate
Sea-kindly	It would be kinder to sail offshore and pull the plug
Good first boat	You'll want to get rid of it at the end of the season
Extra sails	The knackered sails are still clogging up the lockers
Successful club racer	Not worth taking to the championships
Quarter share	You get four weekends sailing and all winter sandpapering

Exhibited London Boat Show 1973	Hasn't been touched since
Ready to sail away	The marina berth expires next month
4-man liferaft	The other two will have to swim
Child-friendly windlass	Seized. Good for drying nappies.

Of course you will also go to boat shows to look at the latest models. DO NOT be tempted to buy one there. In the same way that gambling halls have no clocks and constant daylight, shows are designed to imply that EVERYONE is moving up to 45-footers this year, that it's reasonable to pay only £10,000 more for a blue hull and £1000 is a snip for a new pair of oilies.

Your job is to refine your ideas by looking at all the boats and gear, avoid buying anything, then go home and look for something vaguely similar without needing a mortgage. (With hindsight, the word 'refine' may be a bit optimistic.)

So here are some handy hints on how to be a successful boat show punter.

Firstly, make sure your socks are in good nick, because you will be taking your shoes off a lot as you clamber aboard the gleaming show models (I mean the boats, of course). The last thing you want, when you've just blagged your way onto a 100 foot Swan, is your toe poking out of a hole or a potato showing in the heel.

Another tip is not to wear your best shoes anyway. One mate left his prized crocodile loafers in the basket, only to find a grotty pair of docksiders when

he finished the viewing. (On the plus side they were – of course – the right size.)

Alternatively, you can wear the little padded overshoes on offer. Fair do's, but don't forget to take them off when you leave. You won't cut a dash at the Guinness Bar looking like the back legs of a pantomime horse.

Finding a loo in a hurry is always a problem at shows, particularly after a few pints of the previously mentioned Black Nectar. Don't make the mistake of a (former) girlfriend who panicked, rushed up the red carpet onto a sparkling yacht, checked that the salesman was busy and then used the heads. Hmmm...a tricky one to rectify, with the boat on a cradle and the nearest seawater a day's haulage away.

Once you have passed the sock test and are on board, the salesman will inevitably ask you about your current boat. This is in the same vein as the dentist asking about your holidays. He's not interested in seeing your snaps, he wants to judge how much to charge you: The Seychelles – say £1000 per tooth; Clacton – 75 quid and a free toothbrush. Similarly, the boat salesman doesn't want to hear how you can overtake a Bavaria 32 to windward in Force 2, he just needs to know you're not a time-waster. If you have a Mirror dinghy, now is not the time to mention it. Try something a bit less specific; 'She's a one-off, about 36 feet, hydraulic lift keel. We love her but really need something bigger now we're planning longer trips ...'

Don't overdo it or the salesman may start treating you as a serious prospect and launch into an interminable spiel about every last rivet on the boat: 'This year's model is a little wider and we've used the extra space to stiffen the topsides while still keeping a generous quarter berth ...' and on and on.

Hoist with your own petard, your problem switches to finding a good exit line, or you'll be there all day. Try:

- 'I love the boat but I'm sorry, I can't commit until I've passed my Navigation Theory course. I should get it next time ...'
- 'Would you take my Sulphide Creek One Design in part exchange? Admittedly she needs a bit of work after the fire, but I imagine you could sell her pretty quickly ...'
- 'Of course it all depends on how my shares go. Daddy was a stockbroker when he was alive and still handles our finances via a medium ...'

If all else fails cross your legs and move towards the heads (see above), mention that your wife is nine-and-a-half months pregnant or unzip your anorak to show your Mirror sweatshirt. Smile disappointedly, then leg it.

Back home, resume your research. Somewhere, in a marina in Morocco or up a creek in Cornwall, your new waterborne love is waiting. Armed with the advice above, she's almost yours.

ALL I ASK IS A TALL SHIP, AND A STAR TO STEER HER BY...

The ancients crossed oceans using just a compass and the stars, and today that is still the most satisfying form of navigation. But beware, the compass' apparent simplicity is deceptive – it can be rendered useless by operator error or a bit of iron nearby.

Thor, for example, cocked things up by storing his battleaxe too close to the compass: the longboat missed Poole and ending up at Portland Bill, a poor area for pillage. More recently, Ron's hip replacement gave 20 degrees of deviation on the crossing to St Vaast, causing the crew to miss dinner at the world-class restaurant Fuchia's. Neither was voted man of the match.

But these errors are as nothing compared to our friend John Smith who, on a simple crossing to Cherbourg, somehow got the lines on the compass mixed up in the middle of the night. At dawn he proudly announced 'Land Ho, France ahead! Anyone for croissants?' As we got closer, we spotted a friendly French sign at the harbour entrance. Closer still, and it read 'Welcome to Brighton Marina'. John has been known as Vasco da Smith ever since.

The answer isn't necessarily to go on a course. There you will spend hours converting True bearings to Compass, using sleight of hand based on dubious mnemonics like Cadbury's Dairy Milk Very Tasty', 'True Virgins Make Dull Companions' and 'East West Compass Best'. These do not of themselves guarantee clarity, and can get horribly mixed up in the memory. I once saw a student muttering 'True Virgins Very Tasty' and 'East Milks Dull Companions' as he drew a Course To Steer across the Sahara Desert.

The table below is offered in an attempt to clear up compass confusion once and for all. It's too late for Thor but it may still help Vasco.

True	Word used a lot by sailors in foreign ports
Variation	What sailors look for in foreign ports
Deviation	What some sailors look for in foreign ports, after Variation
Deviation table	I leave this to your imagination
Magnetic pole	Walter, one of our crew from Eastern Europe, who is dynamite in foreign ports
Pedestal	What the ladies put Walter on
Bearing	Walter's attractive stance ...
Handbearing	... although his arm is a bit limp-wristed, to be honest
Datum	Walter's guiding principle
Compass light	Fags favoured by the skipper

'Girls love the aroma of Compass Light ...'

GPS	Generally Points South – the effect the ironwork in the stern locker has on the ship's compass
Swing	See Deviation
Lubber line	Originally Lover Line, i.e. the ship's mobile. Now modified for the Chinese market
Needle	Competitive compass calculations by the crew
Breton plotter	That man selling oysters next to the boulangerie
Compass rose	The female harbourmaster who shows you to your berth

DISTINCTIVE VOICES

A friend was talking the other day about authors' distinctive voices, which led me to wonder how various scribes would have reported the Icon Nationals. First up is the standard report in *Yachting Weakly*.

YACHTING WEAKLY

Twenty seven Icons came to the line in August for their championship at Cromwell Sailing Club. This was a good turnout, buoyed by it being the 21st anniversary of the class.

Light winds greeted the fleet on day one, and in the first race *Nietsche* dominated from start to finish. She was hotly pursued by *Archimedes*, who sadly screwed up on the final beat, so second place fell into *Newton*'s lap.

Day two tested the crews to the limit in a strong westerly, which kicked up a nasty chop. *Darwin* demonstrated the survival of the fittest, and *Gladstone* bagged second from *Caxton*, who pressed her right to the finish.

The final day could have seen any one of five boats winning the event. In a strong southerly *Einstein* set off at the speed of light, but was overhauled by *Pythagoras* who chose the right angle to the windward mark. *Ivan* made a terrible mistake here, colliding with *Hippocratic Oaf* and *Bismarck*, which sank. In the end it was *Lenin*, with her revolutionary new mast, who took the gun and the coveted Madonna Trophy.

MOLECULES MONTHLY

We ask: 'Can scientists sail, or are they too busy carbon dating?'

Match racing, with one sudden-death race, was the challenge Dr Boris Quark had accepted from Castoff, the Russian ace.

Boris and his crew Doris launched *Placebo* into the heavy current. We're on our ohm now, he thought, even the resistance can't help us. He gunned the fuel cell and headed to the start. With his potential energy maximised and uncertainty at absolute zero, he was ready for anything Castoff could bring to the equation.

Castoff streaked out of the starboard box on the Preparatory Signal and pointed his bow straight at Boris. *Placebo* tacked, then gybed, Castoff following closely. Tighter and tighter they circled, each trying to get on the other's transom. 'Now to make use of my PHD' thought Boris and pressed the Depth button three times. Deep below the hull two trim tabs emerged, spinning the boat with radius $x = 2y(p+q)$ onto Castoff's stern. In control at last, Quark carried his opponent out to the right, tacked with a millisecond to go and blasted over the line with the Russian safely covered.

One of Castoff's crew disappeared

below and there was a sound of pumping. Their boat began to creep through *Placebo*'s lee. 'Discharging frictionless polymers', mused Boris. 'Let's see if they're inflammable.' He pressed the speed button twice and a tongue of flame spat from a logo on the port side. Castoff's hull, soaked in carbon-rich liquid, erupted in a ball of flame.

High in an office in Sweden, the Nobel Institute were waiting for the result. 'Has Boris hoisted the spinnaker yet?' barked the chief. His aide twiddled a knob and a screen burst to life, revealing a melee in the cockpit. 'Actually, it looks like he's struggling with a Red Shift sir …'

HITLER

In the master race *Nietsche*, of true Aryan stock, naturally won the first race (pause for applause). She was strong, where the others were weak. I have exhorted her to press on for total domination, and to expand her influence further in the Europeans and Worlds.

Her victory was celebrated that evening by a major celebration in Mein Camp, but afterwards all other parties were ruthlessly eliminated.

SHAKESPEARE

Rough winds shook the darling buds of May as the Bard pushed his new boat, *Avon Calling*, once more to the beach. Sporting the bendy Proctor 2B (or not 2B?) mast they set off for the first buoy, where crew Hamlet remarked 'There is something rotten in the state of de mark.'

Taken fast downwind by the tides of March they overlapped *Yorrick*'s gilden stern at the leeward mark but touched.

'Sonnet!' exclaimed captain S. 'The lady doth protest too much.' And then, quelling all doubts that Shakespeare sailed a 49er: 'Blow, wind! Come, wrack. At least we'll die with harness on our back.'

AFTER SUE TOWNSEND

The secret log of Mole, length 13¾ m

FRIDAY, JANUARY 1ST. HIGH WATER 06.26 4.9M
This is the job list for the winter:
1. I will attend a navigation evening class, and not get diverted to life drawing like last year.
2. I will buy a new almanac. The tides on the ten year old one are getting too confusing.
3. I will buy stuff from the ironmongers, not the chandlers, thus saving 75%.
4. I will stop bodging the loo and buy a new one. The savings on airwick will soon repay the investment.

5. I will plan the season and tell the crew ahead of time where we're going and when.

SATURDAY, JANUARY 3RD. HIGH WATER 07.15 4.7M
Pandora is refusing to crew this year! How my heart beats for her. There is no chance now for the Nationals, or for young love to bloom.

SUNDAY, JANUARY 3RD. HIGH WATER 0812 4.6M
Pandora is threatening to sail with Barry Kent. Barry Kent! The man who was once disqualified for bringing the sport into disrepute for putting ashore mid-race to stock up on fags and beer. And who thumped Mr Gordon, the games master, at the gybe mark when he (rightly!) refused to give Barry room. How can a sensitive girl choose a monster like that over me?

MONDAY JANUARY 4TH. HIGH WATER 0910 4.5M
Now I know why. I tried on my old wetsuit in front of the bathroom mirror. I looked like a badly-stuffed sausage with holes in. No wonder no-one wants to sail with me. How can I get new kit and return to the warm embrace of the one I love?

TUESDAY JANUARY 5TH. HIGH WATER 1005 4.4M
Fred Baxter has come up with a wetsuit from his loft. Although it smells a bit funny, it fits me surprisingly well. He says I can have it for ten packs of Woodbines. I am saved!

WEDNESDAY JANUARY 6TH. HIGH WATER 1100 4.4M
My hopes so cruelly dashed. Pandora saw me in the new kit and said I looked like a morbidly obese sealion. Apparently she and Barry are training every night and tuning the boat at weekends. And she hinted that their relationship is not entirely nautical. I am undone!

THURSDAY JANUARY 7TH. HIGH WATER 1206 4.3M
Sid Jones has offered to crew for me! At least Pandora and I will be on the same racecourse this year. And Sid isn't so bad, provided he cleans his teeth and stops talking about football.

Bring on the Spring Frostbite series, that should cool Barry Kent's ardour ...

STRESS THERAPY

'So, Mr Crankcase, just lie back on the couch and tell me why you've been sent here.'

'Well, engine breakdown is a terrible thing. One minute you're cruising happily, motor-sailing in Force 2. Next the pistons are seized and you're stuck in port for three weeks while parts are freighted and fitted. Even when the repair is made it changes your whole attitude. You're worried about going out of sight of land in case the wind drops and the engine won't start. You practise sailing onto your mooring and get tangled with the boat next door. You go on a diesel maintenance course but realise mechanical things are a closed book to you.'

'I think you're being very hard on yourself. Not many people can fix a diesel. And the marine environment is tough on engines. What is your earliest memory?'

'My mother, head down in the engine room, trying to unblock a filter. I remember screaming in my cot, terrified she'd forgotten to turn off the seacock and the boat would sink.'

'And of course the boat never did sink!'

'Oh yes it did, so often that we called it *The Expectant Submarine*. Mum sent Pan Pans on a regular basis, and more than once we were brought home behind the lifeboat.'

'You don't talk much about your father. Was he a sailor too?'

'Yes ... and no. He always came sailing, but got bored easily and went below to take things apart to see how they worked. Unfortunately they never seemed to go back together properly and we finished each trip with a pile of unused springs and bolts. The yard spent most weeks restoring the equipment ready for the next weekend.'

'What are your feelings now? There's a box of tissues on the table, by the way.'

'Relief every time the engine starts. Dread if it doesn't. A compulsion to change the oil three times a season. Continuous checking of the fuel level. Frequent glances at the water coming out of the transom. I just can't seem to relax. I'm too old for sailing really, but dread getting a powerboat. I'm even considering golf as an alternative ... I'm not sure I can go on like this. I need professional help ...' (pauses to wipe eyes and blow nose).

'I'm sorry to tell you time's up. I think two sessions a week for a year should help but we'll see how it pans out. For next time I'd like you to begin to face your fears. Make a cathartic painting of a diesel and hang it somewhere prominent. Stick pins in it where the injectors go, and the bleed points and the impeller. Repeat until you can do it blindfolded. In the meantime I'll have an engine installed here in the office. In only a few short months you should learn to love it, or at least know where to squirt the WD40. That'll be £100, payable to Screws Nuts and Bolts, Psychiatrists. Thanks. Until next Thursday then ...'

PRIVATE EYESPLICE

The thing about being a private investigator is that you learn to go with your gut.

Take last Tuesday. I was in the office, my size 12s on the desk and a glass of medicinal rye in my hand. In walks this sleezeball by the name of Hiram A Deckscrubber. He looked like the south end of northbound hovercraft to me, but it had been a slow week so I pushed a glass in his direction and told him to spill the beans.

'You got to help me,' he said. 'I'm being blackmailed.'

To calm him down, I asked him what he did.

He gulped the booze straight. 'I'm in the marine trade. I travel in deck hardware. Problem is, it gets lonely on the road. And the wife doesn't like to talk sailing on the phone. Come to that, she's not that keen on boats at any time. But in London I heard about this girl who would come over and talk keel design for a hundred. And for two hundred she'd go over a race real detailed, quoting appeal cases and everything. I called her number. It was some kind of agency, but I didn't care. They sent her over in a full set of breathables. Mid-layer undone to the top of her lifejacket. Hair like she's been in the wind all day. Asked for a pint of Pride, then said she was turned on by anyone who had a choice of downwind sails. Asked if I used a snuffer, you know the kind of thing. A real pro.

'Well, I was hooked. We talked about the advantages of in-mast furling. CQR verses Danforth. Even touched on anti-fouling.

'Once I started I couldn't give it up. One night they bugged the room. Got me on tape arguing about overlaps at three lengths. Now they're threatening to go to Christine unless I hand over ten grand.'

'OK,' I said. 'Get them on the phone. I'll take your case. But it's a hundred a day, plus expenses. And I want trade terms on your whole catalogue.'

The phone was answered by a sultry voice. I told her what was on my mind.

'Sure honey, you want to do racing or cruising?'

'What's the difference?'

'Racing's extra. All the girls can talk fitting out and GPS, but no-one talks the rules like little ol' me.'

We arranged to meet on my boat. I gulped down some black coffee, checked my shooter and hauled my ass down to the marina.

She was late but all that Hiram described. She even had seaweed on her Dubarry's. 'Discipline, Sherlock' I said to myself and poured her a large one.

She got right to it. 'What do you think about tax on red diesel?'

'Cut it, we agreed racing.'

'OK. But let's see your money first.'

I slid her a couple of big ones.

She pushed a couple of forks and the salt into position like they had been lovers all their life. 'I'm this fork and come in late at the windward mark and tack here. This one is on starboard and the shmuck pretends he has to luff to avoid me. In the protest I quote 18.3(a) but the committee don't buy it. Any ideas or are we DSQ?'

We talk back and forth for half an hour. Then I suggest briefing her crew and calling him as a witness, just to see if she'll go for it.

'Yup, I'd get him to say we were on a tack and a length clear when the guy shoved his helm down.'

I pulled out my badge. 'Sorry sister, tampering with witnesses is a Rule 2. Fair Sailing is serious sh*t. We could even get you for Bringing the Sport into Disrepute. You could go down for the whole season.'

She squeezed out some tears. 'Don't turn me in, I only took this job to pay the yard bills. Running a wooden boat isn't easy. The teak decks alone have cost—'

I cut her short. 'OK, get your boss over here and I'll see. It's the ringleader we want.'

She picked up her handheld, flipped to channel 72 and made the call. We sat back to wait.

The boat gave a lurch as the big guy came aboard. He didn't wait to be asked, just came straight down the companionway. I found myself looking down the business end of a handheld flare. I guessed he chose it so he could make it all look like an accident. I've seen what burning phosphorus can do to GRP, and I wasn't about to become another RNLI statistic.

'I found myself looking down the business end of a handheld flare'

Before he had a chance to twist the plunger I reached for the EPIRB and threw it at his head. Stunned, he fought me for the flare. It wasn't pretty but eventually I was sitting on his head holding his arms behind his back. I pressed the DSC red button, then sent out a Mayday on Channel 16.

I told the broad to scarper and held him until the rescue services arrived. 'Nice work,' said the coxwain. 'We've been looking for this little beauty for some time. Little matter of ignoring the Colregs and failing to pick up a Man Overboard. The Coastguard will throw the book at him.'

Later, I settled back into the saloon's deep velour and called *Skimpy's* owner. A blonde, name of Samantha. She could talk navigation all night and that was just what I needed right now ...

THINGS YOU'LL NEVER HEAR THE SKIPPER SAY

- Please.

- Thank you.

- I couldn't have done it better myself.

- You old lags can practise mouth-to-mouth ventilation on me if you like.

- How does GMDSS work? Try it for yourself – press the red button, then press again and hold it down for 30 seconds...

- Bring them all back to our boat. There's a case of vintage champagne I'd like to share...

- Your mother's on Channel 16. Take your time, have a good chat.

- Don't apologise, the gelcoat is always getting chipped.

- Do cover up that bikini, I'm trying to plan our winter maintenance.

- I always do the washing up when I've cooked.

- Cliff Richard? Great, plug your iphone into the cockpit speakers.

- We've a big tank, shower as long as you like.

- I'm quite relaxed about it, we lose lots of winch handles over the side.

- Don't worry about fenders, we'll lie against those greasy old tyres.

- The depth must be on the blink. Ignore it and motor in at full speed.

- Just wave them past, we're not racing.

- A split-pin in the cockpit? No problem, I expect it's from the shrouds.

- Head straight in front of it. Whatever their size, power gives way to sail.

- Tell the crane driver to put the slings anywhere. Our propshaft's really strong.

- Of course we'll turn back. I'm sure your towel is still on the wall.

- Shower together? No, it's very cramped in there.

- No need to slow down under the bridge.

- Oh well, it's only the aerial.

- I don't mind hitting the odd rock, it's upsetting you that worries me.

- You take her in while I furl the main, put out the finders and rig the mooring lines.

- I know it's an expensive restaurant, but dinner's on me. I think you'll like the lobster ...